The

HIS EYE

The Bookkeeping of God

The microcosm in the macrocosm

Gabriele - Würzburg

Christ, the Key
to the Door of Life
Universal Life
The Inner Religion

First Edition, 1999
Published by:
© Universal Life
The Inner Religion
PO Box 3549
Woodbridge, CT 06525
U S A

Licensed edition
translated from the original German title:
"Sein Auge, Die Buchhaltung Gottes,
Der Mikrokosmos im Makrokosmos"
Order No. S 318en

From the Universal Life Series
with the consent of
© Verlag DAS WORT GmbH
im Universellen Leben
Max-Braun-Str. 2
97828 Marktheidenfeld/Altfeld
Germany

The German edition is the work of reference for all questions regarding the meaning of the contents

ISBN 1-890841-14-5

Table of Contents

Accompanying words

God is present, He is eternally streaming light. The All-power of God is also present in shadow, in matter and in sin. A person who strives toward God recognizes the works of God everywhere, even in shadow, in sin. When a person wants to grow nearer to God, he has to actualize and fulfill more and more the Ten Commandments, which are excerpts from the eternal law that God gave to Moses for the people, and the Sermon on the Mount, which Jesus of Nazareth taught the people and also lived as an example for them. Then the shadows recede and the light moves into soul and person.

The one who says that he is a Christian obligates himself before the law, God, to fulfill the commandments and the Sermon on the Mount. When a person strives the toward higher ideals and values which come from the fulfillment of the laws of God, he becomes straightforward, upright and peaceful. Then, he will also respect life and keep peace.

And so, when soul and person strive toward the inner ideals and values and the spiritual-ethical principles, then an inner change takes place in the person - a change toward divine wisdom, toward the knowledge about all inner processes. The actualization of the Ten Commandments and the Sermon on the Mount form the basis for this maturing process; the person grows into the inner life, into the all-wise, divine consciousness. Then he is no longer an intellectual person nor a belligerent person; he is no longer the hero, the power-hungry scientist, the politician who strives for career and prestige; instead, he is the truly wise one who sees everything in the light of the inner life and acts in accordance with the laws of God.

The one who follows the Ten Commandments and the Sermon on the Mount in his daily life strives to recognize and fulfill the will of God in all areas of his life. Only in this way will the person attain true intuition, divine guidance and wisdom.

The wisdom of God has nothing in common with the intellect. The intellect is shaped by learned, that is, acquired, knowledge. On the other hand, the wisdom of God is the intelligence; it is the I Am, the eternal law, God. It is the true Being, the life, that dwells in every soul and every human being. The divine wisdom reveals itself to those people who fulfill the laws of God more and more.

When the wisdom of God becomes apparent in the person, then the human ego, the intellect, diminishes. What takes its place is the All-intelligence, God, the knowledge about all the inner processes of the All, the universe, and about all things. The one who knows the inner processes, the principles of the law which are the basis for all events and things, also knows about the external correlations because he knows exactly what is taking place.

Let it be said once more: A person does not attain wisdom by storing up knowledge - not even if he has read all the books in this world. Knowledge alone does not make one wise. But the one who actualizes the Ten Commandments and the Sermon on the Mount in his daily life matures into the all-encompassing law, God, and attains wisdom. He is then the truly wise one. The one who strives toward this goal in an inner process of developing and maturing is the one whose consciousness expands; this means that the spiritual spectrum he works with becomes greater.

The one who wants to be a being in God no longer allows himself to be restricted by his intellect; he is no longer content with the limitation of his human ego which is intent on constantly striking poses in order to show itself, to make itself noticeable. The human ego sees only itself and knows only itself. This is the narrowness of the intellect.

People who strive toward higher ideals and values, toward the wisdom of God, toward His eternal law, want to bring the laws of God into the world and to renew the world in the Spirit of God, so that there may truly be peace.

Jesus of Nazareth was the greatest reformer. He taught and lived the laws of God and those who followed and follow Him did and do the same. Such people do not leave their lives up to chance and fate. They take their life in hand and master it with the strength that comes from the fulfillment of the commandments of God. They know that the highest power and might, God, controls the All, the cosmic circulation. They live and think accordingly, in order to consciously draw and give from this circulation of eternal power.

People who actualize the Ten Commandments and the Sermon on the Mount are not content to think of themselves as being just a human being. They explore more deeply and, on the path of self-recognition, gain the conviction and certainty that they are beings in God and that every person is the microcosm in the macrocosm. The one who is truly aware of this will not rest until he is close to the One who is the macrocosm - God.

When the divine wisdom opens up to a person, when he is truly wise, then he grasps that everything, even the smallest component of matter, is reflected in the All - that is, it is stored there - and that all changes in the All and in and on the earth are registered in the All. He recognizes the inner correlations of the whole heavenly mechanism - from the pure Being all the way to matter with its countless stars and planets.

Only to the one who matures into the Spirit of the Eternal, into the law, God, is it given to gradually fathom the inner correlations between the microcosm and the macrocosm - for example, how the cosmic person, the microcosm, is in connection with the infinite All, the macrocosm.

Every component of infinity is stored in the All, the macrocosm. The feelings, the sensations and the thoughts of a person are also such components. Likewise, every word and every action is a component that is registered in the macrocosm. Since no energy is ever lost, this energy has to be somewhere and it has to be effective somewhere. It is registered in the macrocosm.

People who immerse more and more into the wisdom of God, into the law of life, experience in and on themselves the pathways that feelings, sensations, thoughts, words and deeds take, where they arrive, how they radiate back, and how they influence the one who sent them out. And so, the truly wise one knows the contents of the components of the All and knows about their effects and consequences.

For, everything gives and receives. All of infinity is based on the principle of sending and receiving, that is, on communication.

Human words are just terms. The one who wants to understand them in their depth, that is, who wants to learn to comprehend the content of the words, has to first recognize himself and find his true self. Only then does he understand the language of the eternal law, which is not the human word as such, but the content of the word, the meaning, the spirit, which is effective in it.

The one who has awakened to the spiritual life, that is, who develops the inner values and ideals more and more, does not take the word literally, but looks for and finds the law, God, in every word. Through this, he looks deeper and very gradually grasps the spiritual correlations of infinity.

People who live in the fulfillment of the law, in God, do not speak from themselves, but the divine in them speaks through them. This is then the enlightenment of the person. When an enlightened person - that is, a wise one - speaks, then his words, too, are enlightened and wise, because they are words that are aglow with the Spirit, words of truth, words of the Eternal and of eternity.

Our sister, who wrote this book, is the prophetess and spiritual ambassador of God. As the prophetess of God, she receives the direct word which speaks to her and, through her, to the people. As the spiritual ambassador of God, she draws from the source of divine wisdom which never runs dry, from the fount of truth in which her soul lives, in order to teach the word of salvation. With her words, which are aglow with divine wisdom, she helps the pilgrims on the path toward the truth to solve their problems and difficulties in a law-abiding way.

The word of revelation, the teachings, the help, the written word - all come from o n e source, from wisdom, from the fount of truth.

In this book, our sister explains the spiritual correlations between macrocosm and microcosm using her own words, in order to give the people who strive to recognize and fulfill the will of God deep insight into the mighty network of communication, into the All-network of "sending and receiving."

Many people want to argue about the word of God. God is truth. The truth cannot be argued, because it is absolute. The one who argues about it grasps only the shell, the word, and not the content of the word. The truly wise one does not argue - he gives. He leaves it up to God and to his neighbor whether or not the word, the help, which comes from the truth, is accepted.

The one who lives in the truth draws from the truth and speaks the truth. He does not want to convince, to prove, to make someone believe - he simply gives. The principle of truth says: May the one who can grasp it, grasp it; may the one who wants to leave it, leave it.

These brief words of accompaniment were revealed by me, Brother Emanuel, through our sister. In the work of the

Lord, I am the responsible servant. I am not a human being, but a divine being, a spirit being, the cherub of divine Wisdom, who stands at the side of the prophetess and spiritual ambassador of God.

Brother Emanuel

A word to the reader

My name is Gabriele. God, the Eternal, calls me His prophetess and His spiritual ambassador. It is not I who call myself this; God, the All-One, has made me His instrument.

For eighteen years, the Eternal has been speaking His omnipotent word through me to His human children, to my brothers and sisters. I am a sister to every person and do not want to be anything else, because in the Spirit of the Lord, we are all brothers and sisters. From the developed consciousness of my soul - which is allowed to live in the All-stream, in the All-One, and which draws from the eternal source, God - I, Gabriele, drew the impulses of life, the eternal truth, and pass them on with my words in this book, for I am a human being on this earth.

Gabriele
October, 1992

The macrocosm of the purification planes and the macrocosm of matter – Splinters from the eternal Kingdom of God

The following statement runs through this entire book, "His Eye, the Bookkeeping of God, the Microcosm in the Macrocosm" like a thread:

Everything and everyone, spirit beings, souls, people, animals, plants and stones form the All and are in communication with every component of the All. Every component of the human body, every spiritual component of the soul and every element of the nature kingdoms is recorded in the stars.

The universe outside of the eternal Kingdom of God consists of the countless stars and planets of the Fall-realms that are of a fine-material type, and of the material stars and planets. The eternal Kingdom of God - the spiritual universes, the seven times seven spheres of heaven - consists of the pure, fine-material solar systems. The whole structure of the All is the macrocosm, which changed through the Fall. Because of the fall of the spirit beings, which wanted to be like God, the following arrangement of the entire universe emerged very gradually.

The eternal macrocosm, the eternal law, the pure fine-material universes, released parts of planets, the Fall-worlds. In this way, the Fall-realms emerged which, after the Redeemer-deed of Christ, became the planes of purification, stations, so to speak, on the way back into the eternal kingdom. During the course of this event, the macrocosm of the purification planes and the macrocosm of the coarse-material planets, that is, matter, developed.

And so, there is the eternal Being, the eternal macrocosm, which is the eternal law and includes all pure beings and the entire pure Being. Besides that, there is the macrocosm with the planets of the purification planes, where those souls dwell that come from the earth after discarding their physical body; and there is the material macrocosm which contains the coarse-material planets, the human beings and the coarse-material nature kingdoms.

The pure macrocosm is the Absolute Law, God, which streams through and maintains all realms and spheres of the All, because God, the eternal law, is omnipresent. Whatever moves outside of the spiritual eternal macrocosm, of the Kingdom of God - the purification planes with their countless finer stars, and the more or less strongly condensed regions, of which matter with its coarse-material stars is a part - are splinters from the eternal Being, the eternal macrocosm, the Kingdom of God. Both macrocosms of the Fall-realms - the purification planes and matter - are part of the eternal macrocosm, the Kingdom of God; they will gain assimilation into the pure Being again.

From this arrangement of eternal macrocosm and conditional macrocosms - the purification planes and matter, which emerged through the Fall-event - the following situation emerges:

The eternal kingdom is inhabited by pure beings; they are called spirit beings. The purification planes are inhabited by discarnate souls and the earth, that is, matter, is inhabited by i n carnate souls, by human beings.

All inhabited planets are surrounded by repository stars. The part of the great whole which was conditioned by the Fall - the purification planes and matter - can be compared to a computer, which I call the bookkeeping of God.

All universes, the pure universes and the Fall-universes, are maintained by o n e power: the Spirit of God, the flowing, omnipresent energy, the eternal law which streams through all things, in which the spirit beings live and by which souls and human beings, too, are maintained.

The two macrocosms conditioned by the Fall – Repository planets for people and souls

The pure spirit beings and the spiritual nature kingdoms emerged from the creation of God, the All-power, the eternally streaming law. The bodies of the spirit beings are compressed eternal law and thus, the microcosm in the divine eternal macrocosm. The spiritual nature kingdoms - the minerals, plants, animals and nature beings - are developmental forms, that is, elementary forms with different levels of consciousness. They are spiritual forms of life, created and formed from the flowing eternal law, God, and are a part of the eternal, spiritual, fine-material macrocosm.

The stars and planets of the purification planes, of which the material universe is a part, are only part-aspects of the pure eternal macrocosm, the Kingdom of God. The planets of the purification planes, where the discarnate souls live, are finer in their structure than the planets of the material universe.

Both Fall-macrocosms, the purification planes and the material universe, adapt their structure to souls and men each time, through the principle of sending and receiving. And so, what a person sends is taken in by the corresponding planets. This is why they are the repository planets for the debits and credits of every soul and every human being. The debit is the guilt, the debt, the inputs stored in the planets. The credit is the cancellation of the guilt in the repository stars and the transformation of this negative energy into positive energy in the soul.

The macrocosm, which is formed by the planets of the purification planes, corresponds in its rate of vibration to the burdens of those souls which live in the purification planes, in order to atone for what they, as human beings, have inflicted upon themselves as sinful. With its burdens, every soul is the microcosm in the macrocosm of the purification planes.

The material macrocosm with its stars and planets records everything that happens on matter. The physical body is thus the microcosm in the material macrocosm, in the material universe, of which the nature kingdoms of matter are also a part. The all-encompassing bookkeeping of God records and stores every component of matter in the Fall-sphere. Every cell of the human body, all functions of the cell structure and of every component of matter consist of different rates of vibration. These arrange themselves and, according to their frequency, enter into the data bank of the purification planes and into the memory of the material universe. This takes place when these processes are already vibrating in the consciousness and subconscious of the person and are thus also recorded in the soul.

According to the principle of sending and receiving, souls and people cannot reach the pure spiritual macrocosm, the Kingdom of God, as long as they are still burdened with heavy sins. On the other hand, the spiritual macrocosm, the Kingdom of God, the eternal law, radiates through all parts which have broken away from it, all the components of both Fall-macrocosms.

All this can be called an absolute registration system. The world of the stars is an enormous computer, which reacts to every occurrence - be it ever so inconspicuous. And so, not one iota is lost, because everything is energy, which continues to be maintained in its degree of vibration as force or form or structure. Every occurrence on this earth, every thought of a person, every sensation, every action, all desires, longings, passions are taken in by these two macrocosms - the purification planes and matter.

Through sending and receiving – A gigantic communication network, a mighty computer system

God, the eternal law which streams through everything, is all in all things, the irradiating, eternal, maintaining and giving power in every component of matter and of the purification planes. The person and also the soul can radiate only as far as their state of consciousness can reach.

The material storage system is closely connected with the memory of the purification planes. Both systems record the causes of people. What soul and person emit, that is, what goes out from them in the form of feelings, sensations, thoughts, words, deeds, desires, passions, cravings and longings - including all previous unatoned occurrences and going all the way back into former incarnations - is received again by soul and person. Through radiation, the sending potential of every soul and every person returns to the person and soul from the computer systems of the two macrocosms and they receive.

As long as soul and person are burdened, they are thus in communication with the purification planes and with the material storage system and are controlled by this world of the stars. When the soul is purified, it is in communication with the eternal Being. Nevertheless, its physical shell, the person, is connected with the material storage system, since all degrees of vibration of the material components of the body are registered there.

Also, the fine-material substance of the different states of consciousness of the life forms of the nature kingdoms - which, in turn, are different degrees of vibration - in the purification planes, the finer macrocosm, as well as on matter, the coarse macrocosm - is carried by the eternal macrocosm. And the coarse-material, for example, the material shell, is directed by both storage principles.

The one who feels into these statements gets a sense of the gigantic and detailed system of registration of God for everyone and everything, which is located outside of the eternal Being, the Kingdom of God.

Neither a soul nor a person can slip through the meshes of this gigantic communication network - the purification planes and the material universe. In order to enter the pure macrocosm, the eternal Kingdom of God, person and soul must have attained purity again. The inputs stored in the stars and planets of the Fall-realms must be erased.

And so, all of infinity is a mighty computer system. I call the pure macrocosm, the Kingdom of God and all positive forces in the negative, the All-computer. I call the splinters of the divine macrocosm, the purification planes and the material universe - the negativity that has attained expression - the causal- or Fall-computer.

And so, we are registered - every single one of us. As long as our souls are burdened, we communicate with our burdens - with both split-off macrocosms, with our own sending potential that is stored there. In this connection, we can also better understand the statement, "What you sow, you will reap." It is the principle: What you send, you will receive.

God is everything in all things. God, the whole principle, the Being, the eternal law, is in every soul and thus, in every human being; for every human being possesses a soul. The incorruptible core of being in the soul is God, the eternal law, the whole. He is the supporting and supplying primordial power in all Being.

The primordial power consists of the seven basic powers of infinity. God, the eternal principle, is in every component of infinity as perfect power. According to the degree of consciousness of the person, perfection, the core of being, radiates one or several basic powers as facets of evolution.

And so, God is indivisible and for this reason undivided in everything - and in everything He is the whole. As a result of this, God is everywhere. God is in every component of matter. In every process, in every event, God is the movement, the life. The energy source of the soul and of the person, the core of being, God, the incorruptible Being, and all positive forces in all components are in constant communication with the pure macrocosm, the eternal law, by way of the core of being. Since everyone and everything is recorded, everything is communication - through the principle of sending and receiving.

The path of the soul to incarnation goes by way of the constellations of the planets

The embodiment of the soul, the incarnation, emerged as a result of the split with God through the Fall, in the course of condensation, of the becoming of human beings.

When a pure spirit being - which lives in the eternal Being, in the divine macrocosm, the Kingdom of God - goes into density for the purpose of incarnating, it passes through the macrocosm of the purification planes and of the material macrocosm, in order to then become a human being on earth.

These paths to incarnation are the paths of recognition for the incarnating spirit being. Thus, in the process of incarnating, the spirit being covers up its divinity with the knowledge about what takes place in the purification planes and how both cosmos, the finer cosmos and the coarser cosmos, react. These steps of recognition for it are stored in the purification planes and in the material cosmos. This is the first magnetism and the first lines of communication which the incarnated spirit being then makes contact with.

The same holds true for either a pure being or for a burdened being which goes from the purification planes into incarnation. The knowledge about its origin and the reason for its incarnation are covered up. Thus, wherever the spirit being or the burdened soul comes from, and what happened there is veiled during its life on earth.

A pure spirit being which comes from heaven and becomes a human being brings with it a divine mission for the earth. A burdened soul which goes to incarnation from the purification planes brings its still unexpiated causes with it, which it should then clear up during its earthly existence.

No matter whether a spirit being or a burdened soul enters into a life on earth, both are led to earth - according to their input potential, which is the same as their communication potential - by way of the constellation of the planets of the purification planes and by way of the constellation of the planets of the material cosmos. Both constellations are largely identical, that is, they are attuned to each other through communication. The constellations, that is, communications, are paths of attraction on which the spirit beings or the burdened souls go to incarnation.

The computer system of the Fall-realms precisely records all processes on the earth and in the soul realms

Whatever happens at every moment in and on the earth, whatever disintegrates and builds up, every stirring and movement of the soul and of the person - in the fine-material and the coarse-material spheres of the nature kingdoms as well - is recorded in the stars and planets. The sequence of the many details which are often only the finest nuances of change, which we people do not even perceive and cannot grasp, is recorded in the cosmos.

When, for example, the skin of a person changes due to the intensive radiation of the sun, then the vibration of the cells also changes and not least of all the atomic vibration of the body. These finest variations are immediately recorded in the computer system of the All - either in the computer system of the purification planes or in the computer system of the material universe or in both.

The causal computer considers not only objective facts, but also the moral-ethical, that is, the inner, components. For example:

When a person unknowingly exposes himself to the intensified radiation of the sun, for instance, while working, or a child at play, then it is possible that the changes in the skin caused by this will be recorded only in the material cosmos, if no serious causes are behind it. But if the person knowingly exposes himself to the intensified ultraviolet radiation of the sun, because he, for instance, wants to bring about a human effect with his tan, then this skin change will have an effect in both macrocosms. On one hand, the thoughts will be recorded in the stars of the purification planes, and on the other, the skin change will be recorded in the stars of the material cosmos.

With every change, be it only in the rhythm of our breathing, we already begin to communicate with those areas of the cosmos where we are registered. Man and cosmos form a unity; for this reason, even the smallest of nuances is stored and immediately becomes active when we change.

Similar processes also take place between the nature kingdoms and the Fall-computers. Strong winds, for example, change many things in nature. When nature is damaged, then these changes appear in both Fall-computers. When plants and trees are destroyed, then the life force recedes. This process also has its corresponding echo in the divine Being.

Every change causes, at the same time, a change in the All. This is the mighty bookkeeping of God - a gigantic computer system.

This inordinately colossal bookkeeping of God is the justice of the Eternal. Nothing is lost - everything is recorded. Every speck of dust, every grain of sand, every atom, every stirring and every inclination, every breath of wind and every ray of the sun, every ray of the moon and every ray of the stars, every sperm and every ovum, every cell of the human body is registered.

In the physical union between man and woman, every sperm which seeks its way to the ovum and stimulates the division of the cells is already guided by the material cosmos. Its path is recorded immediately. If a physical body then develops, it will be registered in the material cosmos from the first division of the cells on. The growth process is guided by the cosmos and, at the same time, the vibration and every movement of the developing body in the mother's womb is also built up in the All.

The macrocosms of the Fall register the death and the birth - the going and coming - of every person, every plant and every animal and accompany the going as well as the coming. Every generation has different rules of life and different forms of life, also in dealing with people and the nature kingdoms; they are recorded and registered in all their details.

The medical, economic and scientific discoveries of a nation and everything that it makes out of this - every feeling, every sensation, every word and every deed - is registered by the Fall-macrocosms. The mighty computer system stores every discovery that is first seen as something ingenious and then dismissed again as an illusion. It takes in and erases and allocates the causes to those people who have manipulated people or nature, that is, have set causes, with their medical, scientific or economic methods.

Every form of life - and be it the smallest microbe which develops very gradually and comes into action - is registered by the material macrocosm and accompanied by the eternal Being in all the movements of its life. Every process of decomposition is perceived by the material macrocosm and is stored, according to the aggregate state it has become. All processes of decomposition in and on the earth, in the water and in the air - and be it of the smallest form of life, which cannot be perceived by the physical eyes - are examined in all their stages by the material macrocosm and registered in their respective positions.

In the same way that a single cell in a life form of nature forms, so, does it also form in the macrocosm. Just as a single cell dies and gradually transforms into another form of energy, that is how the macrocosm registers it.

We can thus conclude from this that every growing component of matter builds up in the material cosmos according to its path of development. Just as each building block of matter changes, so does it also change in the macrocosm. And just as every individual building block of matter dies and goes into another aggregate state - so does the process also take place in the Fall-macrocosms.

Nothing escapes the colossal and just bookkeeping of God. The contents of the countless moments of a day - which each person perceives differently because different impulses are given at every moment for each person - come from the three macrocosms, either from the eternal Being or the purification planes or the material cosmos.

The gigantic and just bookkeeping of God registers all details of life on earth

The human being treats his life as well as the growing life in the mother's body carelessly, and likewise the life and developing life in the nature kingdoms. Many people think they can control the life of another or the developing life in the mother's womb. Many make the earth subject to them in a brutal way and presume they have the right to interfere in the inherent laws of the nature kingdoms. In the last analysis, they interfere in their own life and gradually kill the cellular tissues in their bodies, because they burden themselves more and more by loading themselves with guilt, that is, causes.

Genetic research is being carried out with unimaginable hardness and brutality. Animals and plants have to suffer and die. People, too, are used as experimental objects. Here the person interferes in the genetic make-up of his fellow man and is not aware that he thus burdens himself unimaginably. Who presumes to have the right to manipulate others? Only the one who is manipulated himself and has no respect for life and for the natural course of life.

Today, the abortion laws deal again and again with the question of under which circumstances an abortion should be allowed. When we ask the Absolute Law, then the answer to abortion is a clear no. Abortion is the same as killing; for already when the ovum in the woman begins to divide, a soul whose genetic make-up corresponds to that of the procreating and conceiving parties is stimulated via the macrocosm of the purification planes. The soul which received the impulse through the procreation then very gradually approaches the developing physical body, the embryo in the mother's womb.

And so, the soul brings with it burdens and characteristics of that kind which were active at the moment of procreation - in the sperm of the man as well as in the ovum of the woman. In the soul, which approaches the embryo in the mother's body, also lie the same and like predispositions as those which were active in the sperm and the ovum - either of divine nature or of human causal nature.

And so, it is the parents who determine which soul they attract. What the approaching soul brings with it in the way of radiation-potential - whether positive or negative - corresponds, in turn, to the hereditary material of the woman and the man. Accordingly, the earthly body, the embryo in the mother's body, develops. Every detail of the development or decomposition of a body is registered in the stars, in the material macrocosm.

Now when an embryo - and be it only at the beginning stages of its life - is aborted, then an approaching soul is driven away; this means that a developing body was killed and a soul was denied incarnation. These causes fall upon the person responsible. Everyone concerned is allocated that amount of guilt with which he took part.

It is incomprehensible to our human intellect that all details of life are registered. But the gigantic and just bookkeeping of God is the result of the All-principle: What you send, you will receive again.

Everything is contained in everything - this is why everything is stored. Even every blood vessel, the composition of bones, muscles, tendons, ligaments, of the lymph, lymph vessels and the lymph track, of glands and hormones - every smallest component is recorded. All the processes in nature, even every movement of a tree, a bush, a plant or an animal is triggered by the stars and again registered.

The guidance of God then takes place by way of this absolute registration in the material macrocosm and in the macrocosm of the purification planes. The decisive factor for a soul which incarnates is how much light or shadow it brings with it into this world. For out of this results the indirect or direct guidance of God.

According to its shadows, a heavily burdened soul is c o n t r o l l e d by the purification planets via the material macrocosm. It cannot be directly guided by the eternal Being, by God; for it lives in its human self-dynamics. This means that it creates more and more causes and is oriented to its shadows. Such a person lives, as it were, in a prison, whose bars were created by his human ego. He communicates only with his causes, in the end, with the stars in which his ego is stored.

The indirect guidance is the maintaining and impulse-giving energy. It is the wake-up call of God. Because of unalterable principles of the law, the All is constantly in motion and through this brings the causes to their effect, which the person has to bear as illness, fate and the like - if he does not follow the divine wake-up call. The person will be controlled by his own burdens, until he awakens and higher recognitions gain a place in his life.

Let us become aware of what a mighty cosmic clockwork is ticking, in which every person is also a small wheel that, according to how it meshes with the whole mechanism, runs faster or slower or is erratic or stands still. When in a quiet hour, we think about these exact correlations of the three macrocosms and about the absolute bookkeeping of God in the purification planes and in the material universe, then we comprehend why we are on earth. And that is to become divine again in order to return as a pure being into the eternal macrocosm, into the eternal divine law. The one who becomes engrossed in these explanations also understands the statements: “Even the hairs on your head are all numbered.” “Are not two sparrows sold for a penny? And not one of them will fall to the ground without your Father’s will.” (Mt. 10:29-30)

Impulses from the stars of the computer systems guide the soul on its earthly journey

In the purification planes where the souls live, there is a constant coming and going of the souls by slipping in and out of the flesh. The joining of soul and person takes place with the first cry of a newborn - this is the soul's slipping into the flesh. The soul that incarnated in the small child now has the task to prepare the body it has accepted for its earthly existence.

Every soul has its life-rhythm, its special vibration which results from the light and the shadow of the soul. A light-filled soul, that is, one which is not very heavily burdened, has a harmonious rhythm and thus, harmonious movements. A burdened, that is, shadowed, soul is characterized by disharmonious rhythms and disharmonious movements. The soul conveys these rhythms, these vibrations, to its physical body. For this reason, each child has different movements already from its birth on.

The first cry of the child is, at the same time, the first exhaling and inhaling of the soul in its earthly body. This first contact with its body, the first cry, is different with every newborn, because this first breath of the soul in the earthly garment shows the soul's degree of vibration - either harmonious or disharmonious.

For the soul, the first cry in the physical body is the docking or coupling, so to speak, with the earthly body and, at the same time, in the union of soul and body, it is the first input into the stars for the new earthly life. At the same time, it makes contact with what it has stored in the Fall-computer which it - if it was incarnated before - has left there from previous incarnations.

Again and again, the soul of the human child receives impulses from the computer system to make human sounds, impulses which urge it to listen to sounds, that is, to the words, of the parents and members of the family, in order to learn the human language, so that it can make itself understood in the course of its growing and maturing.

The soul incarnated by way of the planet constellations which corresponded to the contents of its soul. These constellations contain the life programs for this journey on earth. In this way, the new citizen of the earth is already in contact with the causal computer, with the two macrocosms, which are the purification planes and the material cosmos, or with the All-computer, the eternal macrocosm - depending on the lights or shadows of its soul.

The cosmic computer system also gives the newborn the impulses to open its physical eyes and to sharpen its hearing. With the help of the soul, which receives the impulses from the stars, the eyes in the physical body open; the child gradually begins to see, to hear and to understand.

The little person has to learn to see, to hear and understand. In this, he is helped by the cosmic computer which activates the programs that are stored for the soul in the planet constellations. The family and the people who surround the newborn also contribute so that the soul is very gradually able to penetrate its not yet programmed shell, the physical body, so that it can be either guided by God, the eternal law, or controlled by the purification planes - depending on what the soul brings with it, light or shadow.

And so, the decisive factor is where the soul comes from, from light-filled heights or from the regions of shadow where it lived as a burdened soul. In the small citizen of the earth, the soul prepares its body for the rest of its earthly life, day by day, week by week, month by month, year by year. The first life programs for its life on earth emerge during this phase of preparation. To the same extent as the body reacts, that is, sits, stands, speaks and moves, the soul slips more and more into its body and branches out there. It is as though it works its way into its body, in order to master all the functions in the growing and maturing body, until its physical body reacts in a mostly synchronized way to the soul. Through this union, an interaction between soul and body develops - both have an effect on each other.

The gradual slipping-in of the soul can be compared to a tree that is growing its roots. Just as the young tree gradually works its roots into the ground and spreads out its root system, it is similar with the soul which very gradually permeates all the fibers of its earthly body with all the vibrations of its being.

The physical body – The mirror image of the soul

No soul can exist without the incorruptible energy, God. And this is also true for its shell, the human being. Therefore, the human being is made up of spirit, soul and body. The spirit is the incorruptible energy, the core of being of the soul. The words "core of being" mean that it contains the divine heritage, the mentality and the capabilities of the pure being. The core of being is in constant communication with the Kingdom of God, with the eternal macrocosm.

The soul is made up of spiritual particles. The spiritual particle structure bears in part the burdens from past incarnations. With these burdens - that is, shadows - the discarnate soul in the purification planes or the incarnate soul, the human being, is in communication with those planets in which the programs of its burdens, its causes, are stored.

The one who interferes in the great cosmic event of an incarnation, for example, by aborting an embryo, will one day have to endure the same or something similar. In one of his next incarnations, the same fate will possibly catch up with his soul. It, too, will be pushed back through abortion, or it will incarnate in a so-called underdeveloped country under inhospitable conditions, because it once denied a being, a soul, its development on earth.

The physical body is the mirror image of the soul. The radiation of the soul is the result of what it acquired in the different incarnations, in its different physical bodies. This is what the soul radiates into its physical body; this is what marks the soul. And so, what the soul bears, light or shadow, is what it transmits to its shell. With these vibrations, it brings into action the atomic structure of the human being, who is then portrayed in the same way as the soul radiates.

For this reason, the earthly body is also called a thought-body, because the thoughts of the person are the reflection of the light-filled or sinful soul. The radiation of the soul is based on what the person has entered into his soul via his feelings, thoughts, words and actions, via his desires, his passions, his longings - or via the fulfillment of the divine laws.

The light of the soul brings out in its physical body that the person is noble, fine and good, that he is for his neighbor and with his neighbor. The shadows cause spitefulness, envy, animosity, intolerance, arrogance, vanity, belittlement of one's neighbor, addiction to pleasures and much more.

For the most part, the person and his soul are a unity. The radiation of the soul is the same as the radiation of the person. This radiation-intensity connects soul and person with the cosmic computer. The light-filled soul communicates with the All-macrocosm, the eternal Being. The burdened soul and equally burdened person communicate with the macrocosm of the Fall-realms, where their sinful programs are stored.

The material macrocosm is the memory bank for the movements and processes on and in matter. It also stores the sinfulness of the person which his soul, after the death of its earthly body, then takes into its new person, if it happens to incarnate again.

Light and shadow have their effect on all components of the physical body. By way of what is stored in the All, a cause in the soul can therefore become effective in the person as illness, as fate and the like, because every cell, every component of the physical body has a part in the programs of the human ego.

The soul in the person is on a journey. By way of the causal computer, it is controlled and guided to those places where it is to recognize and clear up its humanness. It is also brought together with those people with whom it has to clear up its former contrary way of behavior, its sinfulness. In manifold ways and means, the attention of soul and person are drawn to the still present sins, so that the person can recognize them in time, in order to clear them up with his neighbor, through Christ, before the causes break out.

We are on earth to become divine

And so, we are on earth to become divine. Each of us is in the school of life called earth in order to learn to recognize himself and to clear up his sinfulness, so that this is erased in the soul and in the computer system of the purification planes. Through this, the negative energy transforms into positive energy in the soul - soul and person again establish communication with the core of being of the soul, with the eternal Being. After its physical death, the purified soul can then return to the eternal home, from where it went out as a being of light.

The path into the eternal Being takes place according to lawful processes. Every soul and every person has free will. According to its free decision, to either burden itself more or to cleanse itself from sinfulness, the soul goes either into the purification planes over and over again and to further incarnations, or it goes back to the eternal home.

The Eternal, God, gave mankind the Ten Commandments through Moses. Jesus of Nazareth taught us the Sermon on the Mount. The Ten Commandments and the Sermon on the Mount are inherent laws of the eternal macrocosm, excerpts from the eternal law. These rules of life hold true for people of all faiths. They were given to us so that we may apply them in our daily life, so that our soul can find its way to its divine heritage and return to its origin.

Only on this path of the actualization and fulfillment of the commandments of God does the soul become more light-filled, the person happier, healthier and wise. The path of turning back and of entering into the origin of the true Being has the effect that soul and person find their way to the truth and the person becomes truthful. This shall be the goal of every soul and every human being.

The physical genetic make-up draws the soul into incarnation once again

The soul of the one who does not master his life-task to become divine again will then incarnate again, when a part of its stored causes becomes active in the material cosmos and in the cosmos of the purification planes. These causes then draw the soul to incarnation. The condition necessary for this is that the inclination is present in the soul either to want to experience some things again as a human being or to expiate its sins, or to continue to work on a worldly task which the soul could not finish in a former earthly body, because physical death caught up with its earthly body.

The urge of a soul to go to earth can have genetic reasons, when people procreate a body whose genes bear causes which are connected with the predispositions of that soul. For instance, if this soul as a human being was a scientist who had worked with several scientists on a discovery, then the tendency of the soul to continue to work as a human being on this project can be very intense.

Scientists who have worked together on a discovery, for example, on space projects or computer technology or gene technology or splitting the atom have a common group karma; for everything that is against the law, God, binds those souls to each other who worked together on this task as human beings.

Computer technology is against the law of God, when people are kept under surveillance and controlled by computers. It is then possible that these scientists continue to work together on their invention in another incarnation. What they have begun in previous incarnations is in their hereditary make-up, in their genes, and also in their soul.

According to the principle "like attracts like," such people come together again in further incarnations - in different earthly bodies, but with the same genetic make-up. When the specific hereditary predispositions become active, for example, regarding the invention of computers, the manipulation of genes, space flight, the splitting of the atom, extensive surgery and so forth, then the souls which have incarnated again begin to expand further and to test their plans.

When this so-called ingenuity is against the law of God, then these people are controlled by interest groups outside the earth, by souls which have the same predispositions as the incarnated souls, the human beings. And the Demons' State, too, devotes its attention to such and similar discoveries. Its motto is: Everything that is against God is welcome.

If a soul does not gain insight or understanding in a future incarnation, it continues its work on what it brought with it, for example, on gene technology. Then, the person will also enter its new achievements and experiences into its soul and into the astral computer system. When, after the death of its body, this soul incarnates again, it may possibly bring along again all that it has learned as a human being in previous incarnations. The body and its genes are then also formed accordingly.

And so, it is possible that a soul continues to expand its negative life programs over incarnations, that is, over generations, until one day the causes become effective and it reaps what it has sown - perhaps over centuries.

The human being takes itself very seriously as a person. In reality, he is only the capsule; we could also call it the garment, or the shell, which encloses the soul. This capsule-like existence, "person," consists of the sinfulness, the humanness. The sinfulness of each person is, so to speak, his physical genetic make-up. Everything that corresponds to the human ego, including the physical hereditary material, came forth from base feelings, sensations, thoughts, words and deeds, also from passions, longings and excessive desires, the wanting to be and to have.

The whole complex of the human ego, the density, seen as a whole - matter - I also call the person-law. It is the capsule in which the soul and the spiritual power, God, are found.

What a person has stored in the computer system is never the same as the inputs of another person, just as one person does not look exactly like another. The day, too, is for each person his personal day, because each person feels, thinks, speaks and acts differently every day, because each has different desires and inclinations.

And so, every person is individual in his nature and therefore is also called the individual who has his particular characteristics and peculiarities; they are the particular character of the individual. It is the law of the individual, also called the person-law.

The person is thus marked by what he has entered into his soul and into the memory bank of the computer system. This is what, in turn, also controls him. The sum of the wrong behavior of all human beings is called the causal law, which forms the causal computer.

The whole of infinity is sending and receiving – Communication

Thus, the whole of infinity is law. There is nothing other than law. The pure Being is the Absolute Law. Both macrocosms that were caused by the Fall - the purification planes and the material cosmos - are the causal law, in which every person, every soul and all coarse-material forms are stored. Every person has the free will to live in accordance with the excerpts from the eternal law, the Ten Commandments and the Sermon on the Mount, or to create his own law, his personal law, his individual law.

According to the principle of sending and receiving, every person calls up that with which he is in communication through his radiation. When soul and person are in communication with the divine, they receive health, peace, happiness, harmony and inner joy, because the eternal law is selfless love, peace, joy, harmony and happiness. It is the Being, eternity, infinity. When the person emits hate, envy, animosity and strife, then he will also reap in turn what he has emitted. When hate, envy and strife come back to the person as compressed energy, as focused radiation, he becomes ill, suffers or starves and does not find peace anymore.

The eternal law radiates throughout the spirit beings and the pure nature kingdoms, which became pure form out of the eternally flowing law, that is, they became compressed eternal law. The spirit beings live in the stream, in the eternal law, God, and receive from the eternal law, which is the selfless love, the perfect Being.

In soul and person is also the streaming energy that remains, however, the maintaining life force, until the human being turns to God in his inner being, fulfilling the laws of God, so that the maintaining energy is able to stream through soul and person more intensively. A part of the positive energy was reversed in polarity by soul and person. The human laws, which soul and person have made for themselves, are their person-law. This is active in them; this radiates through them; this marks soul and person; and this also comes back to them.

By means of the cosmic communication, the pure beings are given the possibility to come into communication with all pure forces in the All - including with the pure Being in the various material forms or in the souls - since all is contained in all things. Every pure form of life is compressed eternal law, which is its spiritual heritage - the infinity. Since each spirit being is compressed eternal law and, at the same time, bears within the whole of infinity as heritage, it is absolutely free, also in its movements through infinity. It is bound to no place. All paths to all stars, to all planes of heaven, are open to the pure being, because it is compressed law in the streaming, eternal law.

To say it with other words: Every spirit being is given the whole of infinity as its heritage. For this reason, it is in communication with all the inherent laws of God and by means of the spiritual gravitation, it can move everywhere, for like always attracts like. No area of infinity is distant and inaccessible to the pure one, since everything is in all things and everything, the fullness of infinity, fills and streams through the pure one.

On the other hand, the burdened soul and the burdened human being can send and receive only as far as their sending potential, their consciousness, reaches. The soul in the purification planes can move only as far as corresponds to its limited consciousness, that is, as far as its radiation, its communication, reaches. Its radius of movement, too, is in accordance with its radiation-potential.

The physical body, the human being, is a product of the earth and thus can move freely only on earth.

The decision for God and the fulfillment of His laws – or for our own law

In all of infinity, nothing happens by chance. And so, it is not by chance that a person lives in a certain country and in a certain place. As a human being, the soul lived in this place in a previous incarnation and had built up a negative magnetism which, in turn, is registered in the stars. This magnet, which can consist of many different causes, has drawn the soul to this place which the person calls his home. For the incarnated soul, for the human being, this adopted home should be a place of recognition and expiation. The person will experience much at this point of reference. Those occurrences and experiences which take place there can also be connecting points to previous incarnations or indications of burdens in this earthly existence.

Soul and person are thus on a journey. At the place where they live - on the earth or in the purification planes - they should recognize and clear up some things, in order to transform the magnetism, the negative energy, into positive energy.

Every person stands at a crossroads every day - for or against God. With every feeling, every sensation, every thought, every word and every deed, we face the decision: Do we want to think humanly or do we want to fulfill the commandments of God?

To decide for God means to fulfill the laws of God. To decide against God means to act against the laws of God and to create one's own law, the person-law. Every day, we either build up new programs, which are then also registered in both computers of the Fall-realms, or we communicate with our already existing programs. We ourselves can observe this; our whole life tells us. It consists of our feelings, sensations, thoughts, words and actions. Because of these programs, we are in contact with what we have entered into the macrocosms and we behave accordingly.

Communication in the Fall-computer system – The law of sowing and reaping

Let us remember the following: Just as each one of us radiates, so does he receive. This is what communication consists of.

The All-communication-network is the eternal law, which is contained in everything, also in matter. The one who fulfills this law is free, since he is bound to nothing and no one. On the other hand, every burdened person is an individual computer; for he feels, senses, thinks and speaks in accordance with the sending potential which he brought with him, his self-made programs.

In the eternal kingdom, it is said: Unite and be. On matter, the demonic reversal - divide, bind and rule - predominantly holds true. The principle is always the same - sending and receiving.

Our world is the miniature of both computer systems of the Fall. In our world, too, everything has to be recorded, that is, registered. Let us think of the bookkeeping in business, of the registration of a newborn baby or the permission to reside in a country, when we want to stay there for a longer period of time, and the like.

Every human being is registered many times, from birth until death. When a soul looks upon the light of this world, that is, when a child is born, registration begins. When was it born; what is the child's name; what are the parents' names; where does the child live; where do the parents live? When the child has grown up, questions are presented to the adult about his profession, place of residence, family status and so on. When we want to live in another country for a longer period of time, then we are asked: How long and why? The registration for every person continues until death: Died on ..., when and where? And so, every person is recorded and registered by the administrative system.

The registration on a small scale indicates that there must also be a large scale registration - the bookkeeping of God in the All. There are no mistakes in the bookkeeping of the Eternal, in this great computer system. At every moment, everyone and everything is measured, weighed and recorded by the corresponding stars, all according to their radiation. This bookkeeping, this registration, takes place day and night, at every moment - until everything negative has transformed into the positive and can again be taken into the circulation of the fine-material, into the eternal Being.

The regeneration of the material nature kingdoms, the minerals, plants and animals, also takes place on sections of the purification planes. The part-souls of the animals, which have adopted many a human aspect, have to give this up in certain regions of the purification planes. The human habits of the animals, above all of the domestic animals, will be allotted to human beings as burdens, not to animals.

The earth has an important function to fulfill in the mighty complex of the purification planes and of the material universe, for it is the transit station for all burdened souls in earthly bodies.

In the course of certain rhythms, both macrocosms, the purification planes and the material universe, radiate - rain down, so to speak - negativities, that is, causes, onto matter. These causes then become active in and on the person. But every person is allotted only his part - those causes which he has entered into the computer and which are also in his soul.

We could compare this outflow of causes to the rain coming from a cloud which brings the stored water onto the earth. The outflow of causes and the simultaneous intake of the sending potential of human beings, minerals, plants and animals is a circle within the range of activity of the causal computer. This path of communication, the sending from the earth and the radiating back from the repository stars is the law of sowing and reaping: We receive what we input.

A model for the earthly computer: the cosmic registration

Man has developed the computer in our modern time. Where does the knowledge come from about computers, which are used by specialists in almost all businesses? How did the knowledge develop about this small storage system which many people use as a matter of course in this technical world?

It began already in former times, when the contrast between rich and poor began. The more unscrupulous a person was, the more he attained and became rich at the expense of his neighbor, who then also let himself be subjugated by him.

It is not much different in today's world. The wanting to be, to possess and to have, the greed for power and prestige, increased right up into our generation, but now we justify what we have attained today with our system of law and let our might and our prestige speak.

The rich one first took slaves whom he made work for him. Their salary was a meager meal. The next steps were the servants who were hardly any better off than the serfs, the slaves. They, too, were granted only a paltry salary. Then there were the people who were the vassals. They worked the land for the great landowners and in part, they, too, were serfs.

Then, as government structures developed in time, which demanded taxes, a form of registration became necessary, because the principle of a state to which tribute had to be paid developed more and more. In order to be able to keep up the state system, a suitable registration had to be developed and carried out. It answered the questions: Who has paid and who is still in debt? In this way, the first two columns of bookkeeping emerged: the debit and the credit.

Through this reversal of a part of the eternal law - from eternal Being to wanting to be, from divine heritage to wanting to possess - emerged the debit and credit. This externalization brought with it the striving for outer riches. Through this, the negative sending and receiving potential developed: divide, bind and rule.

The rich and those who wanted to become rich cleverly worked out more and more precise registration possibilities, in order to be able to record everything and everyone. They were helped in their thinking by those souls in the purification planes who had insight into the computer principles of the Fall-realms. Step by step, they reflected images into the people as to what this computer system is and how it can be used on earth.

What was reflected by the souls was reduced by the people to the common denominator of their needs. What crystallized out of this was a bookkeeping of the people with its bookkeepers. There were big accounting journals with incoming and outgoing entries, with debits and credits. The first accounting journals were written by hand. In later times, came adding machines which were already making things easier for the bookkeepers.

Through this image reflection from the soul realms, the computer system for this world then gradually developed as technology advanced.

A bookkeeper who serves a large corporation with his energy is surrounded by much technology in today's mechanized world. For over the course of time, big businesses with large accounting departments have developed from the simplest of enterprises and small businesses. This system of calculation, posting and accounting consists of computers. Every business is interested in saving on people and time. For this reason, the advantage of technology is used.

The person who has familiarized himself with such a network of technical processes sees and hears how technology can be put into motion and controlled with ease. Machines calculate, post, add, enter, store, register and keep the data in their storage systems, for example, on computer discs.

Thus, we see that what is in the All was reflected down to earth and absorbed by some people. It was applied to matter so that it could serve the wanting to possess, to be and to have. But there is one thing that technology cannot replace: the exactness and conscientiousness of a bookkeeper. The bookkeeper, and not the machine, is responsible that all entries are entered in the proper column, that the debits and credits are correct. He has to know in which system and in which memory bank each file is entered and recorded. And so, the bookkeeper has to be able to master and operate the machines, for they don't work on their own.

In earlier times, it was enough that the bookkeeper could calculate, post and keep an exact accounting journal, that he knew about the individual accounting procedures and could substantiate them with the help of his accounting journal. At that time, good carbon paper and a good accounting pencil was required. In today's mechanized world, the bookkeeper has to know about an entire accounting and computer center. His task is to know the functions of the computers and to know, for example, on which discs the accounts are stored and also how he can erase or reproduce them.

Our generation lives in the world of technology as if it were second nature to them. In this world, there is a specialist for each technical area, who can instruct us in the use of the highly sensitive equipment and machinery.

The macrocosms of the purification planes and of matter are a modification of the All-computer, of the eternal law. The eternal law is eternally existing. The Fall-law is the causal law, the registration of all that is against God. Further modifications are the computers of man, which cannot function without a bookkeeper and qualified experts.

The Fall-computer, that is, the causal computer, was very deliberately created by the one who wanted to be like God. It was done by reversing the divine and pulling down the positive into the negative, the contrary. With this work of "divide, bind and rule," the demons have set their own trap; and because of their own inputs, they, themselves, are gradually falling into it. The one who closely observes the trend of the world, the signs of the times, recognizes that this trap is already in the process of snapping shut.

In addition, what the demon introduced on earth as a product of ingenuity - the retrieval from the Fall-computer of man's computer with bookkeepers and experts who use it - is all caught in the trap; for these achievements, too, served and serve those striving for power and possession. It was and is used to force man into the yoke of bondage, in order to one day make him completely into a slave, into a spineless tool of a so-called new world rule.

As in earlier times, the mighty of this world also use their servants today - now it is the computer "servant" - to force their subordinates, their "slaves," into the yoke, to keep them in the yoke and to exploit them even more.

The discerning man of today asks himself: Why is all the available data on every citizen registered in a gigantic memory bank? Why, with the help of gigantic computers, is it seen to that every citizen of the state - including every church Christian in Germany - pays his taxes down to the last penny?

In many businesses, the work of every employee is exactly recorded down to the minute and kept available by computers. The slave holder of the past centuries could not check down to the very last detail what his subordinates produced for him as work and profit. But the industrial magnate of today can record exactly the performance of his conveyor belt worker, as well as of his star salesman. This knowledge can then be used to decide, for instance, whether a worker stays or is fired.

This is an example of so-called progress in the course of human history.

The exactness of the Fall-computer is the justice of God and - in accordance with the principle "you will reap what you sow" - leads man via self-recognition into freedom, if he clears up his sinfulness; or it leads him into his fate, if he continues to build upon his wrongdoing.

On the other hand, the computer of the earth's technology registers people in order to then admonish or fire them according to the consciousness and interests of the magnate. In this sense, it is a tool of "divide, bind and rule."

The Fall-computer registers everything that takes place on earth. No person and no soul can return to the All-principle, to God, unless they have cleared up t h e i r negativities down to the smallest detail. Since the causes come more and more quickly toward people as effects from this Fall-computer - that is, causal computer - the trap of evil is closing. The souls will then remain in the purification planes, in order to there expiate through suffering what they did not want to recognize and clear up as human beings.

Ideas, discoveries and inventions can be retrievals and the control from the regions of the beyond

The one who has read the first pages of this book carefully is aware that nothing can emerge from nothing; there must be something already there from which it was or will be derived. The small, mechanized world was derived from the storage system of the Fall, from which aspects, the small building blocks for the technology of this world were taken, for example, for the human invention of the computer.

The knowledge about the mighty, cosmic storage system is in the soul of every person; for the soul, itself, the microcosm, is the compressed All-computer in the mighty All-computer of eternal Being.

How do retrievals from the Fall-computer system come about, which enable man to design and build a machine? As though out of the blue, an impulse comes into the brain of a person who is, however, guided or controlled by a power – either by the divine principle or by souls from the astral worlds.

For example, when a person wishes to be a great inventor and when he has the corresponding predispositions for this in his genes, then his genes are stimulated by his wish. The programs, a part of his physical genetic make-up, begin to emit, because the person has entered this idea, his wish to become a great inventor, into the memory bank of the purification planes and into the material storage system; the person then receives.

This impulse, that is, the idea for a certain invention, can also come from an energy field which he himself built up in previous existences and which is based on the wish to be a great inventor. It is possible that several people have once worked on the fulfillment of such a wish-picture and that their thoughts went into the storage system. The impulse, the idea, can also be retrieved from the programs of this sending potential.

It is also possible that the wish to be an inventor is fulfilled by souls which make so-called injections into the communications of the person. When this happens, then the thought to be a genius intensifies in him. For instance, it could be souls of former human beings with whom, in one of his previous existences, he has worked out certain programs that then went into his soul and also into the causal computer, via the principle of sending and receiving. In this incarnation, the wish-impulse now comes from the souls of those who were once his co-workers, as well as from one of these energy fields which were created then. Thus, his thought processes are stimulated twofold and guided in the direction of that project which he wanted very much to carry out.

There is also the further possibility that this energy field, which he himself has once co-determined, and which now wants to determine him in return, is controlled by interest groups. This means by groups of souls in the spheres of purification, which want to make him, the human being, into their tool, in order to reach a certain goal through him. By way of a telepathic impulse, he is then persuaded that he has to become a genius.

The person is addressed via the magnetic field of his desires, so that he begins to think more and more. He has idea after idea, concept after concept; one thought builds on the other - it becomes an entire chain, a whole network of concepts.

And so, he creates more and more images, that is, programs, in his brain - for example, how a computer can come into being. The control from the beyond continues. Idea after idea, detail after detail - more and more images emerge in the world of his thoughts.

On the basis of the many impulses, he gradually constructs a machine over the course of time, for instance, a computer. First he has only put parts of it down on paper. They now tell him how he has to go on building. The pictorial concept and what he has already put on paper are the magnets through which those in the beyond stimulate the person again and again to seek and to research, to use this and that detail and to incorporate it in his technical work.

It is also possible that the interest groups of the beyond lead the person to scientific books, from which he can take further impulses for his invention, for his work. In this way, piece after piece of the puzzle come together, so that in time an entire picture emerges and from this the construction of the machine.

Based on his wish to be a great inventor, he receives ever more and ever deeper impulses, that is, information, from the different sources in the beyond, by way of the principle of think and receive, that is, sending and receiving.

The world of technology emerged to a great extent through such controlling. That which is laid out in infinity in an all-encompassing way and for the good of the whole was reversed more and more in the Fall-computer and, via the Fall-computer, on this side of life, in this world - and, in many cases, it was done to the woe of mankind.

Impulses can also come to man from the divine. They are helpful, selfless impulses for selflessly serving people who do not strive for their personal aggrandizement, but give honor in the world to the One who gives the impulses. They are then for the good of all people who are willing to fulfill the will of God.

Clearing things up with Christ leads to becoming free of egocentric programs from previous incarnations

Every human being is in the school of life called earth. Sooner or later, every person - depending on how the constellations of the stars stand in relation to the inputs in his soul - is stimulated to think about his life, that is, whether or not it is consonant with the Ten Commandments and the Sermon on the Mount. When such or similar impulses do not come in this life, then the struggle with one's own sin begins in the spheres of purification - when the soul is discarnate and lives in the beyond.

From this, one can conclude that a life without difficulties, without being rattled and shaken, is not necessarily worth striving for. For the impulses which stimulate us to self-recognition and to overcome the negative, come in particular from the disharmonies in our life. The days of our earthly life are measured - and they are precious, because we can clear up so much in one single day. This is why it is said: Use the time!

Everything that does not correspond to the eternal law, God, the mighty All-computer, has to be recognized and cleared up. The individual cannot recognize from which constellations, that is, channels, the impulses for self-recognition come. But when he wants to learn about his sinfulness, he has to go to the levels of his own feelings, sensations and thoughts and be willing to honestly look at himself, in order to recognize himself and to clear things up.

An impulse which, for instance, calls attention to our negative thoughts and egocentric wish-pictures can also reach us by way of a shock, which moves us for a longer period of time. Through this shake-up, thoughts may be triggered that show us what the reason is for our wanting to become successful, famous and rich.

When in this incarnation the wish emerges to affirm oneself, to prove oneself, to gain prestige and power, then these are hints that possibly there already had been the same or similar thought patterns, from which causes were created during previous existences. These causes may be activated in us again today and stimulate us to continue in this epoch to work on the project that we had begun in previous existences. And so, now on this side of life we contribute, for example, to the further development of a machine.

What comes to us via telepathic paths is nothing more than thoughts which we believe to be our own. In order to find out whether or not there could be negative influences at play, we only have to get to the bottom of our thoughts, our desires and emotions. Every one must examine what he wants to achieve for himself with these thoughts, with his intentions and whether the thoughts that come up in him are in accordance with the Ten Commandments and the Sermon on the Mount.

When we have applied the criteria of the Ten Commandments and the Sermon on the Mount to our way of thinking and wanting and when we want to free ourselves from these impulses that influence us and which come to us via telepathy, then what we have to do is set out exclusively the Christian path, for Christ is the way, the truth and the life.

No one can free himself from his humanness - this is possible only with and through Christ. The path of the transformation of these negative, sinful programs into positive, divine life means: Repent, ask for forgiveness, forgive - and do not commit the same again.

Even when we do not know whom we should ask for forgiveness, God knows about all things. When we accomplish this reversal of the human wanting and doing with the Spirit of the Christ of God in us, by refraining from what is non-divine, then we will also attain forgiveness and liberation from our sins.

Every one has to go this path - scientists, inventors, theologians, statesmen, rich and poor; no one is exempted from this. Every human being and every soul has to become conscious one day of what this means: Every feeling, every sensation, every thought, every word and every deed sends and receives.

Every person is a computer, a sending and receiving station and, at the same time, a memory bank that, in turn, stores everything that he sends out. And so, there always has to be a program, a counterpart, in us. Only then can we retrieve from the computer system and perhaps continue to build on this program.

When there are programs in us, we recognize this by the fact that our thoughts move and irritate us. Let us become aware that no energy is lost. Everything we input, and be it only o n e thought that we think, returns to the sender. What the person makes of this depends on his world of feelings, for this is the gateway to the soul, to the programs stored there and it is also the gateway to higher or lower forces.

The words of Jesus were in the following sense: Just as above, so also below. In the eternal Being, in God, in the pure heavens, there is an absolute law-communication of the absolute powers of God. Outside the pure Being, there is the communication between souls and souls, souls and people, and between people and people. Whatever programs the individual has in his soul, that is, whatever he sends out - he is in communication with the same or similar frequencies.

Impoverishment of the human being's spiritual energy through the reversal of the divine life force

Since God, the Eternal, created His children from His All-power, from His streaming Spirit, the eternal law, they are compressed eternal law and thus heirs to infinity. They possess all the powers of infinity and live in the fullness of infinity, because the infinite is the fullness.

The one who turns away from the All-power and creates his ego-law will also receive only according to the smallness of his thought processes. For many people, this means that sooner or later they will live in need and infirmity or in suffering and illness.

As already described, every being which separated itself from God received a quantum of positive life energy from the eternal fullness. He is called to bring this quantum of borrowed, divine energy back to God, into the fullness from which he had received it.

But when soul and person walk the path of sin and when the person has thus largely used up this quantum of divine energy, he will become impoverished and live in need. Suffering and illness, too, show that the person has mostly reversed the positive power which was given to him. The one who drowns out the warning impulses which preceded the suffering or illness, or the warning impulses in the suffering and in the illness, by accusing others that they are to blame for everything and continuing to have the same behavior which led to the loss of energy, will, in the course of time - on this side of life or in the beyond - just simply vegetate away or fall into infirmity.

When the opponents of God, the demons, are interested in a person, they will do everything to make him submissive to them, by redistributing negative energy. For this, they take a part of the potential of other people and transfer a quantum of it to the one whom they have chosen as a tool. He could be, for instance, an inventor or a scientist. Through this influx of negative energy, he is brought onto a life orbit, onto an ellipse where he is sustained, and upon which his causes cannot catch up with him so quickly.

The demons redistribute these negative energies exclusively to people whom they want to use - that is, misuse - for their purposes. Such people can then remain healthy and live far into an advanced age, because negative energies are radiated to them over and over again, which, for the time being, shield them from the effects of their own causes.

But sooner or later every cause has to be borne, including those causes that people created with the negative energy redistributed to them by the demons, in order to perhaps carry out in this world what the opponents of God need to keep their territory. The reversal of this borrowed, divine energy, which every person himself carries out, forms the person-law. This egoness-law is the negative, which every individual himself has created through the satanic principle of mine and me, the wanting to be and to have.

A sign that a person is becoming more and more impoverished in divine energy is, for instance, the showing-off of his person, the exposing of his human ego, the currying of favors in the hope that others reinforce him in his thinking and abilities, the claiming of power or the wanting to be looked up to, the acquiring of goods and money or the wanting to become a great inventor, in order to have power, in order to acquire wealth and prestige. That is the principle of mine and me - everything only for me - the wanting to be and to have.

God is the fullness, and the one who lives in the fullness of God and lives in God does not need to reach for the fullness as a human being. However, the one who becomes more and more impoverished in his soul, because he reverses the borrowed, divine energy into negative energy, reaches out for might, prestige, wealth and the like.

The earthly heritage: riches, possession – The confining, personal ego-world. From binding to connecting

Through the impoverishment of the soul, the person limits himself increasingly and becomes more and more oriented to this side of life. He then sees only his little world and his human heritage. The one who turns away from the divine heritage, from the divine fullness, wants solely for himself. He wants money and goods; he wants property and to possess; he wants wealth and prestige; he wants land and a house; he wants a wife for himself and she wants a husband for herself. Both want children for themselves. Each one creates his little world for himself and separates himself more and more. Through this, he reveals his egocentricity and demonstrates to what measure he is spiritually poor and spiritually destitute.

The human heritage is the evil spawn of sinful feelings, sensations and thoughts, out of which emerged the me and mine, the wanting to be and to have. Because human beings have distanced themselves more and more from the divine and thus have become impoverished in spiritual power, many must earn their bread by the sweat of their brow or earn the bread of the "rich." The "rich one" takes his subjects, his slaves, so to speak; today they are called employees.

In this way, the differences between poor and rich developed. The rich one on earth thinks he is rich and uses these riches to make others dependent. But personal wealth points to inner impoverishment. The one who does not use his wealth for the good of his neighbor will sooner or later also lose externally what he wanted to keep for himself.

However, every person has the chance to become rich again in his inner being through the actualization of the Ten Commandments and the Sermon on the Mount. In this way, he again reverses with Christ the negative, the transformed-down quantum of borrowed positive energy, into the pure life energy that he received from God to take along with him.

Every single one journeys toward his origin again - but when and how, is determined by each person, himself.

And so, we recognize the impoverishment in the mine and me, in the wanting to be and to have. How often do we hear: "I have acquired this or that with much effort. What I have acquired," for example, a piece of land, "I'll fence in so that my neighbor recognizes my heritage, but can only look over the fence." The person calls this confinement, the "smallness," which one is not allowed to enter, his heritage.

Through the sinfulness, the mine and me, through this impoverishment, the thinking in terms of "lots" developed. And so, many people create their little world, their lot. They then call this their property.

When death catches up with the person tomorrow, then this lot is no longer his property. Consequently, it cannot really be his own today either; it only seems to be his possession, for he has to leave it behind. But the sin, the impoverishment of his soul, the reversed quantum of borrowed, divine energy, he takes with him into the soul realms. This is his individual law, his sending and receiving potential. This potential of his sins is the beam of his consciousness and knowledge. This is how far the soul can think and see now, and only so far does it see its path in the purification planes.

Thus, each person has entered his sending and receiving potential, his path, into the memory bank of the stars. He is in communication solely with these inputs. This is his small world. What the individual has entered into the stars is found to a great extent also in his genes.

What a person is tied to is written in the stars. The input in the causal computer is also the binding.

For instance, when we consider our house to be our possession, then we are bound to it. With the death of our body, we take this binding with us into the purification planes. It is registered in our soul and in the causal computer.

Jesus of Nazareth said: "What you bind on earth shall be bound in heaven, and whatever you loose on earth shall be loosed in heaven." (Mt. 16:19) We now understand the so-called bind and release commandment. It means that whatever we bind through our wanting to be and to have remains bound on the earth and also remains registered in the stars of the macrocosms of the Fall. What we release by way of realizing something, repenting of it, asking for forgiveness, forgiving, making amends and by way of a firm will to no longer do it will be released on earth as well as in heaven.

It is not the eternal Being that is meant here with "heaven," but the beyond, which is often figuratively called "heaven." In heaven, nothing can be bound. It is the purification planes where that remains bound which the souls do not let go of. This is then also bound on earth, in this world - always in those who want to hold on to it, and also in the stars, where their sinfulness is stored.

That which remains bound on earth is, at the same time, the magnet, which again draws the soul to this side of life, to incarnation. That which is released in "heaven" - that is, in the purification planes - is a step on the path to the true, eternal heavens.

What results from this is the fact that the commandment of binding and releasing, which Jesus of Nazareth gave to

His followers holds true not only for the apostles, the bishops and theologians, but for every one - person and soul - who wants to lead a Christian life, that is, who wants to actualize the commandments of God, the ethics and morals of the Sermon on the Mount. It is not given for just a few people, but for all.

The commandment of binding and releasing is never a mandate for forgiving sins through a third person, for example, through priests. Christ is our Redeemer. Since He, the Spirit, who dwells in us as power and light, is the transforming and redeeming power in our soul, we can release what we bind on earth only with Christ. This means that the release cannot take place simply through a so-called auricular confession.

We alone can release it, for we were the ones who bound it. How should a priest release it? As a person among people, he has to recognize and clear up his own bindings, which we, in turn, cannot release for him.

And so, the release of a binding is done only through the high priest, the priest of all priests - Christ in us. He is the Redeemer of all souls and men. When we repent with all of our heart for the bindings we have created, we go with this sincere, deep remorse to Christ and will take the path that He has shown us.

The steps to release are: We recognize the binding, we repent, ask for forgiveness, forgive, make amends for what can still be made good and no longer commit that sinfulness. Instead, we fulfill more and more the Ten Commandments and the Sermon on the Mount.

The one who, in this awareness, goes to Christ in his inner being receives the true absolution through Him. The burden is released through the transformation of the negative energy into positive, highly vibrating power. This erases the records in the soul as well as in the stars and in the genes and thus, in every cell of the physical body. This is how we go, from binding to connecting with the divine, the eternal law in us.

Negatively thinking and acting people – Energy-suppliers for the hierarchy of the demons on this earth

By inputting the negative and through the reflections of these inputs, the spiritual body of Fall-beings enveloped itself. We call this garment which surrounds the soul "human being." The physical body is a divine concession; it developed very gradually through the reversal of the positive energy on loan.

The path of the soul in a human being should be taken consciously as the path back to the origin of the pure being, to the eternal fullness, God. The soul is immortal. After the death of its physical body, it goes into the purification planes, into those worlds toward which it has thought and spoken itself, in accordance with the quantum of reversed positive energy.

In the purification planes, which were called the Fall-realms before the Redeemer-deed of Christ, there are regions where those Fall-beings, which are not willing to turn back, live and work. They place themselves above God and have founded their hierarchy in order to go against God. They are the demons.

This world with its countless satanic establishments is the main base of the demons. By "world" is meant the dispolarized human being with his technical achievements, who acts against the law of God. The "world" is not the planet earth, but solely what is created by people and is not consonant with the laws of the Eternal.

The hierarchy of the demons on this earth, in this world, is maintained by the negative energies generated by people and the redistribution of the same.

Because of their unlawful behavior, many people can be influenced by the demons, so that they then fulfill the demonic will. Those who daily feel, think, speak and act negatively, that is, who reverse their positive potential into negative energy more and more, are the energy-suppliers of the demons. From many of these sources of energy, they take negative energy again and again, which they use according to their plans, for example, for scientific inventions, for the development of gene technology and the like.

Demonic control of the human being according to his negative genetic material: telepathy, besiege, possess

The demons strive to preserve their hierarchy and expand it. With the reversed, that is, demonic, energy, they influence and control those people who are active and work for them, according to the principle: Send negatively and you receive demonically. The control takes place solely in accordance with the human predispositions, with the genetic material, the physical heritage of the individual.

The soul may have already brought with it its present negative potential from previous incarnations, when this was not cleared up as a human being or as a soul. The hereditary material consists of genetic components, which bear what was inherited from parents and ancestors.

Who, for instance, can the ancestor be? Perhaps the same soul in the human being of today, which once lived as a human being in another generation. Today that person in the ancestral line is the ancestor of the human being. And so, we can become our own descendent and be our own ancestor.

Whatever the soul bears, the genes bear, too. The soul, that is, the genes, urges the human being of today, who was the ancestor in the family tree of the family, for instance, to become an inventor, because he had already worked on an invention in a previous life. The hereditary material of parents and ancestors is a part of the genetic makeup of the newborn; for the law says: Like attracts like.

And so, the components of the hereditary predispositions of the human beings attract again and again that soul which corresponds to their characteristics, that is, to components of their hereditary predispositions. Based on the law "like attracts like," and through expiation with those who have the same or similar burdens - the same souls come together over and over again, only in different human bodies, in order to clear up what they have caused.

The soul realms are spheres of expiation, where all feelings, all sensations and all thoughts become visible, which the soul once felt, sensed and thought in the earthly garment and were not cleared up by the human being. Nothing is hidden there, because the soul, from the beginning of its discarnation, is in the cycle of expiation.

On the other hand, the incarnated soul, the human being, still lives on the sphere of expiation and probation, the earth. Probation on earth will exist only as long as leading souls back is still possible from the earth. Much is hidden to the human being, because he conceals his thoughts and like gives rise to like again and again. The hidden, often glossed over with the word "mystery," is nothing more than the sinful, the evil, which we hide for good reason, because we would otherwise be ashamed of it and it would give rise to a corresponding reaction in our fellow man. After the death of our body, all this is apparent.

During his life on earth, the previous incarnations of a person's soul are covered up, because the energy of the day, which is a part of his Fall-energy, shows him the situations and events that he should clear up today.

The causes which lie in the deeper layers of his subconscious are hidden to the person - only their effects become visible. Just as the tree is hidden in the fruit of the tree, so are the effects hidden in the causes of the person. These become apparent when the stars stimulate the seed. Therefore, the day is given to the person, and for each one, this day is *his* day; for each day shows each one certain aspects of his causes which he should clear up today, in order not to have to experience the effects.

On earth, the human being has the chance to make amends for what he has caused. In so doing, he does not have to go to his neighbor and clear up with words and gestures what he has spoken toward him and done to him in thoughts. On earth, he can do it in silence, by way of his thoughts, by communicating with the soul of his neighbor through Christ and clearing it up.

On the other hand, in the spheres of purification, the feelings, sensations and thoughts are apparent. There, we have to clear up with the soul of our neighbor what happened in secret on earth, because the hidden thought becomes visible in the beyond. Then only expiation is possible.

A soul can come to the earth as a soul, in order to be among human beings. The result is that souls can possess people, if their state of consciousness is similar to the state of consciousness of the soul. But a person cannot go to the soul realms to be among the souls. Human beings cannot possess souls, because souls are invisible to people. The human being, on the other hand, is visible to the soul.

The contrary beings in their demonic regions are not yet in expiation, because they live from the negative energies of human beings. The demons - like souls - can come to earth, because their body is in a finer aggregate state. This finer substance, of which the soul bodies, too, consist, can also make use of a human garment - when the latter is in the same or like state of consciousness as the Fall-being with a finer structure.

To make use of a human body means to besiege or to possess it. While doing so, the soul of the person is pushed aside. In this way, interest groups of souls, for example, former doctors or former scientists, who as human beings once began a certain scientific project and did not finish it, can influence people by way of their genetic makeup. Their goal is to induce them to carry out those deeds which the interest groups of souls could no longer carry out on earth - either because no opportunity for this was offered to them or because technology had not yet advanced far enough.

Whether or not we fulfill the conditions to receive telepathically or to become besieged or possessed depends on our motivation, our sending and receiving potential. Our own sending potential, that is, our state of consciousness, is thus the decisive factor for whether or not we can be influenced.

When the person is power-hungry, when he craves prestige and wealth, then his motivation will not be the fulfillment of the will of God, but he will want to do something for himself, in order to attain what he longs and strives for. If he has the chromosomes of an inventor, whose predisposition is only toward power and prestige, then it will not make any difference to him whether or not the earth is exploited or the magnetic field of the earth, the earth-dynamo, is disturbed by a technology that he develops.

Many say that the end justifies the means. When we look into our world of feelings and sensations, when we look at ourselves more precisely, then we will recognize ourselves and learn what we want to aim for. Every day, each one of us has to ask himself the question: Do I want to be guided by God, or do I want to be controlled, besieged or possessed by souls?

Our life, our feelings, thoughts, words and deeds tell us with which range of frequencies we are connected. Each one of us will one day be weighed and measured, and declared accordingly, at the latest as a soul in the spheres of purification. No one can escape the memory system; each one is registered and - in accordance with the law of cause and effect - each one has to account for his feeling, thinking, speaking and doing, before the mighty, eternal law, God.

Building so-called achievements of technical progress over generations

We cannot say: Forgotten is forgotten. The assumption is erroneous that a matter is "buried and done with" if the fuel of humanness in it dwindles and gradually disappears. Inputs can exist for millions of years and even longer. In the bookkeeping of God, only what is cleared up by the individual is erased and transformed. Inputs entered at the beginning of the condensation of matter can still be retrieved, when a part of these old inputs suddenly becomes active in the genetic material.

Knowledge and technology, including technical accomplishments of ancient times, can be called up in the memory system of the two causal macrocosms via activated genes, in order to then continue to research and construct more on the basis of this knowledge. In this way, not only the knowledge multiplies, but technology is improved as well. If these technologies are unlawful, for example, gene manipulation, then the demons, too, have their share in it; for they want to reduce their territory, the earth, to their denominator.

And so, much comes to us human beings via retrieval and telepathy, and much is demonic, that is, it can come from the sources of demons. People who have scientific experience and knowledge stored in their genetic material can, over generations - because the souls come again and again - in each case retrieve only a part of the knowledge. But over the course of the generations, these pieces fit together like a puzzle and in time result in a completed whole. Then in one generation, the so-called ingenious invention results: People construct cleverly thought-out machines, for instance, a well-functioning computer, whose blueprint was borrowed from the principle of the causal computer, where all the stirrings of people and all the movements in the nature kingdoms are stored.

Atomic research was carried out for a long time. Then came the time when the atom was split and processed. Again and again, the same souls go into the earthly garment and continue to build on their research or inventions, until the human, so-called ingenious, achievement, for example, the nuclear power plant, has been developed.

In the same way, genetic research, too, developed over a few generations, until finally some scientists put together the puzzle of gene manipulation.

Everything that is against the laws of nature - for example, animal experiments, gene manipulation, splitting the atom and much more - is against the eternal laws of God. What is against the All-law, God, is satanic and comes back to mankind as effect. Through the many excesses, by which the earth and everything on the earth were maltreated, the earth now suffers from the causes of the people, and the people suffer from their own self-made causes.

A look around in our time tells us: This world is moving toward the abyss. Mankind is determined to reverse all divine energies on loan into negative energies. Through this reversal of positive to negative energy, also emerged airplanes, vehicles, satellites, space shuttles and much more.

Even though the world already stands at the edge of the precipice, in the laboratories people still think and do research and in the industries of the world things are still tried out and built - all with the negative energy which will ultimately bring mankind to its downfall.

The final spurt is announced. What was already tried out in former generations is, in many cases, retrieved again from the stars. It is thought about further, that is, it is further researched and further expanded. Whether we can still actualize all mental acrobatics of the human ego, depends, in turn, on the two macrocosms that were the result of the Fall.

The delusion of man that he, himself, is Creator and God

Many people, especially our scientists, think that no limits have been set for them. Many people feel that they are above God and are of the opinion that everything is manageable and feasible. Here I am thinking of a new, repeated "Fall" of sin, the manipulation of the human hereditary makeup. The "ingenuity" of the human ego even wants to create a new human being and a new nature as well. In the final analysis, this means a new world, because the old world is no longer able to exist. The influence of genes is chosen as a means to accomplish this. And so, many are striving - above all those in government and the scientists - to create a new order according to the demonic principle: divide, bind and rule; enslave the people and subdue the earth in a cruel way.

In this highly mechanized world, many believe they are the greatest. Unscrupulousness has no limits anymore; every one is rapacious and greedy and the one who asserts himself seizes the power and rules entire nations; and the one who is at the helm turns the people into industrious, paying slaves, who even pay for the maddest follies, for example, genetic engineering. In this way, entire nations let themselves be manipulated, that is, they let themselves become more and more enslaved.

Man has destroyed the life of mankind and of the earth; for everyone and everything has fallen ill as a result of the effects of the human ego, the wanting to own, to be and to have. Through the use of genetic engineering, man believes that he himself can now be Creator and God, by relinquishing the reins for his life to the power-hungry. He thus lets himself be controlled by the manipulators.

It is therefore possible for the power-hungry of this world, the manipulators, to control nations, because in the end every person wants to go sky-high with his ego, in order to gain as much as possible for himself, personally. Because everyone wants to save his property or increase his possessions, he can be manipulated and, for instance, be incited to war. Every war brings destruction, plundering, killing, murder, exploitation, enslavement and much more.

Since everyone wants to control only with his ego and to make a profit of it, everyone also enters his causes, his base ego, into the computer system. This means that the genetic material of man becomes worse and worse, for the causes have their effect on the body. The demon has also recognized this and now wants to create a new human being with a new genetic material which is in accordance with his own ideas. In these newly shaped genes, there will also be a component which makes man submissive and a peaceful slave, who carries out what the power-hungry one wants – in the last analysis, it is the demon.

The spirit of false gods, egocentric man, thus wants a new heaven, a new earth and peaceful people – but such that do what the demon wants. With this, he tries to reverse the words of the Eternal: a new heaven and a new earth. The demon says: "By way of gene manipulation, I create a new earth and a new heaven." For then, just as the manipulated slaves would think and behave, a new causal computer could develop, that is, a new heaven, a "heaven" of the demons.

Man, himself, brings about the end of this world

God does not let Himself be mocked. All these demonic aberrations will grow to excess; for every human being, every soul has to sooner or later recognize whom he has served and who he was - including every demon.

God, the Eternal, loaned positive energy to His human children, but did not deliver it entirely into their hands. What came from the law will again flow back to the law.

The time has now come when hardly anything more can be brought into motion, because the motive power, the positive energy, is lacking, since this loaned energy is mostly used up, that is, reversed into the negative. This means that the film reel of the human ego, the waste of energy, will be rewound. Every one, whether man or soul, has to watch the film of his own life.

The world is falling apart, because its structures do not hold together anymore. Illness, pestilence, infirmity and hunger are sweeping the people away. The destroyed ozone layer of the earth, the ultraviolet radiation, the polluted rivers, lakes and oceans, the lower quality of food, which hardly contains the necessary nutrients anymore, that is, life force - contribute to the fact that soon man will no longer be able to exist on this earth.

Now, the only possibility left to the demon is to transfer negative energy from here to there, that is, to shift it from here to there, so that some people may be successful every now and then, causing many people to hope that things will continue as they are or that they could even improve.

But this shifting of energy is possible only to a certain extent. It will no longer continue in this way, when the effects of the causes that people have set and still set come faster and faster. Then, even more people will suffer from their effects, including those who want to keep the world ship on course, through tighter and tighter earthly laws and through manipulations of various kinds.

The one who suffers and wastes away hardly has any more motive power to determine or explore anything; for he is now the prisoner of his causes which have become effective.

Even though everything in this world is turning topsy-turvy, many demons and many souls and people - most of all the scientists and, in their following, theologians and ruling authorities - are still of the opinion that they have conquered God. For God does not interfere in the Fall-event and does not put an end to these doings. God sets no end to this human activity. Man himself will accomplish this, because every one has entered his end and the end of this world into the computer system of the law of cause and effect.

The condensation of the Fall-beings into human beings began with the head. The brain – a conglomeration of Fall-programs

A great part of mankind today still lives in a dream-like state - they think that the gods of this world, the "great ones," can do everything. Many of these "gods" and their patrons are still of the opinion today - through the principle of divide, bind and rule - that they can increase their power, their prestige and their influence. For many, the repository planets of the material cosmos are t h e i r planets, which they can explore and maltreat. For many, the divine breath of life is their breath, t h e i r life.

Another category of people is of the opinion that God does not exist, or that, if there were a God, He would be a weakling, because He endures everything patiently.

Most people are unable to realize that through the principle of sending and receiving - that is, of cause and effect - this world is falling apart. The human-demonic power structure thus says: "divide, bind and rule"; this is a declaration of war against God.

To be able to understand the unreality, the Fall, we have to start with reality, with eternal Being over and over again.

God does not interfere in the downfall of this world. Every person, every single one, has to turn back and with the help of Christ transform the negative energy into positive energy. This is possible only through the actualization of the divine principle, of the eternal law, which consists of equality, freedom, unity and brotherliness. Each one is equal to the other. Every one is himself responsible for everything that he senses, thinks, says and does. The one who does not accept these principles of the law scatters and destroys, because he is a destroyer. He has a destructive effect on his own life.

How long the fight against God will continue cannot be expressed in years. It already began in the heavens - through the Fall. We know that as a result of this, the ever more condensing - that is, becoming ever coarser - Fall-realms, all the way to the coarsest structure which is matter with its earth, emerged from a part of the fine-material eternal Being.

Just as the Fall developed, all the way to matter, so will it return - from matter into the fine-material, into the pure, into the eternal Being. The supernovas which are known to us today show how the Fall took place: Out of the supernovas emerged, via turbulences, all the solar systems of both macrocosms, which in time became the dwelling planets of the Fall-beings, including human beings. To the same extent that the structure of the Fall-beings became more coarse, the structure of the part-planets, of the Fall-systems, also condensed.

The condensation of the Fall-beings into the human body began in the head. The first conglomerations of Fall-programs developed in the head; today this conglomeration center is called the brain of man. Starting from this center, from the developing brain, the fine-material body began to grow coarser. The cell structure developed from some spiritual particles and, via this cell structure, the organs of the human body were formed.

The spiritual body folded itself to the same extent that the physical body was formed; this means that its particles folded into each other. In the beginning, the brain of the human being in development was very primitive. The being, which was transforming itself down through its wrong behavior into the developing human being, could not yet grasp what was happening to it.

Today it can still be said that the human being is the brain; for as he feels, senses, thinks, speaks and acts, so does he react and so is also the make-up of his body.

Many people are proud of the performance of their brain, of their intellect. Especially through so-called "brain-oriented thinking" much damage was and is done in this world. The person whose thinking and living still takes place today on the level of his intellect, in what is stored in his brain, does not yet grasp that he is destroying himself through the Fall-law, called the law of sowing and reaping.

Through his ego-programs, the human being is a reversed, programmed being. I call this whole complex of the human being density, which emerged from the divine energy, was transformed-down and now has to be reversed again, from negative energy into divine energy.

The reel of his fate, that is, his own film reel, will one day be rewound for each person. Each person will have to look at himself as an actor, so to speak, who plays his own role in each life picture. The pictures, in which he himself is the main actor, consist of what he, the human being, is himself as well - of his feelings, sensations, thoughts, words and deeds, of his passions and longings.

What is condensed, dispolarized, needs again the lawful polarization, the restructuring from the human to the divine. The path to reach divineness again is the same for everyone: whether poor or rich, whether big or small, whether high or low - everyone will walk this path. It consists of deep remorse, asking for forgiveness, forgiving, making amends as far as this is still possible, and no longer committing the sinfulness.

The Christ of God, the Redeemer-Spirit, stands at our side on this path. Only through Him will we find our way back into our Father's house, by playing back our human ego-reel, our own film reel, and by dissolving it.

We do not need to seek God in far away places - the omnipresent power, God, is everywhere; it is in every spiritual particle of our soul, in every cell of our body, in everything we see. And so, God is thus life that is present.

Since God is the core of the positive life force in everything, also in what is condensed, reversed and transformed down, the new, positive life grows out of the negative - through Christ, the pushing and pulling power, the transforming and redeeming energy.

By turning away from God, the Fall-beings created the conditions for life on earth

God, the eternal law, serves all pure beings and helps all souls and human beings who turn toward the Eternal, God. But the one who turns away from God in the belief that he himself is a god capable of doing anything will sooner or later have to earn his bread by the sweat of his brow - when his causes come into effect.

The being in the pure Being, which lives in the law-stream of God, works creatively in the will of God, the law. The impulse of its will is the creative "Let there be," with which it helps to arrange the heavenly worlds, in service to the great Creator-Spirit, the eternal Father, whose power brings forth everything.

The genius of the human ego still believes that it is creative, since it wants to be like God: a creating spirit that can do all things on this earth - for the good of its human ego, but not for the good of mankind.

The Fall-beings and the emerging human beings were also subject to this delusion. They believed that they could create and form in the Fall-worlds just as they did in heaven - all according to their will. Only very gradually did they become aware that now they had to earn their living, their bread.

In the same way, the genius of the human ego, too, will have to become aware that it can be neither creative nor able to shape and form; the gift of God on loan, the positive energy, is mostly used up, and what can still be formed with negative energy is limited. Then, what developed, that is, what escalated, on the earth over billions of years is finished: The arrogance of a humanity far from God, which thinks it is placing the holy, divine, giving principle in the service of demonic-human egocentricity.

The present generation does not think much differently than the first Fall-beings. It, too, wants to possess and to have and is not aware of its indwelling energy, the power of God.

The first Fall-beings had to realize that their creating and shaping abilities could not bring forth anything lasting and fruitful, because they had turned away from the Absolute Law, from the serving and selfless love.

The Fall-beings, which gradually changed into a dense structure that we today call matter, suddenly felt what hunger meant. Their developing material body needed to be supplied with dense energy. Very gradually, they began to hunt and to cultivate fields. They hunted because they had chased themselves - namely, right out of paradise. Hunger drove them to catch prey. At the same time, they began to eat the herbs of the earth. Later, they cultivated them in order to have nourishment for their physical bodies.

Let it be said once more: God takes care of His pure children. The one who turns away from the law of purity, who creates his personal law, the Fall-law, has to take care of himself. The body that became denser and denser needed more and more energy, and the body that is now dense, man, cannot have enough of it.

Because man has turned away, and today still turns away, from the energy source of life, God, he sought and seeks to cover his ever growing need for energy, wherever it seemed and seems possible for him. Unscrupulously, he took and takes for himself what came and comes to mind, he seized and seizes, robbed and robs, and exploited and exploits.

And so, after countless periods of time, it came to what we have to recognize and experience on our own body today: a polluted and ravaged earth, poisoned rivers, lakes and oceans, a destroyed ozone layer and nutrient-poor food. The results are hunger, epidemics, need, disease, blows of fate and much more.

Since the genetic material of man, of animals and of plants now suffers under the causes of the human ego, this means that the genetic material has mostly degenerated; man now wants to become creative again, in that he believes that with the spirit of the times he can create a new heaven and a new earth - by changing the genetic material.

Man destroys himself and his environment. The cup is full. Now there is only, "either – or"

God, the Eternal, has arranged life in the eternal Being in such a way that everything is in communication with everything. The nature kingdoms cannot exist without the spirit beings and the spirit beings cannot exist without the nature kingdoms. It is a great whole which forms the unity of God, a working together and a flowing of forces into each other.

The same holds true for man. The person, who is a body that comes from nature, cannot live without nature, and nature, in turn, needs man. Just as the spirit beings work in the law of God in the pure Being, so should the law, the Spirit of God - the creative shaping and maintaining principle - become effective on earth through the children of God, the human beings. Everything is a great whole, a mighty communication network, a weaving and meshing in the great unity, God.

Those who violate this unity, this mighty communication network, will have to suffer under their causes and eventually also become impoverished. Because the insatiable human being wants to attain more and more, and live even better, he interfered and interferes in the great cosmic communication network, God, in the pure energies that were given to the Fall-beings, in the harmonious weaving and meshing which comes from mighty Spirit, God, who holds all things in His hands and maintains all things in His hands.

The ignorant human being became a cannibal. He hunts the animals, kills and consumes them. The ignorant human being also tortures the animals and destroys nature. In this way, he falls more and more into spiritual derangement - the constriction of human egoism - and into inner impoverishment.

All of mankind is now on this precipitous path. Now the lifeline is supposed to be gene manipulation. Gods want to create *their* new heaven and *their* new earth for themselves. But God, the only One, the Eternal, keeps His spiritual work in His hands. Density will pass away. Man destroys himself; the base humanness, everything that has emerged through the violation of the law of pure selfless love breaks to pieces and will be transformed.

The laws of God will once again build up that which was and is in God: the new heaven and the new earth - with a new human race that lives the eternal laws.

So God also gave His rebellious children the nature kingdoms, which, along with the Fall-beings, became denser in the course of the Fall-event. Nature and the fruits of the fields, meadows and pastures should have served the emerging human beings and later on the human beings as joy and communication and nourishment as well.

The one who is not aware that God holds everything in His hands destroys, manipulates, and wants his own heaven and his own earth. Over the generations, many people were kept blind and also let themselves be kept blind and be led blindly, because they paid attention only to their own good and disregarded that which is their life, nature.

The majority of people are still blind today and thus have not realized that every person, himself, shapes his life through his feeling, sensing, thinking, speaking, wanting and acting. What he sends out as feelings, sensations, thoughts, words and deeds is what he receives again. And so, he will reap what he sows.

By turning away from God more and more decidedly, many people lost the knowledge about their spiritual, eternal homeland, as well as the awareness of their origin, of their divinity. They also lost the knowledge that they themselves were the divine microcosm in the eternal macrocosm and that they still are so, deep in their souls. They are not aware that they are a part of the eternal order, of the Kingdom of God, and that the connection of their innermost being to God cannot be destroyed or broken.

Even today, many people still live in similar ignorance as the Fall-beings, which lost the knowledge about the communication with the infinite One and with infinity. Many do not believe in God or are of the opinion that God is far from them; they are not aware of the might and power of God. Many may very well speak of God and pray to Him - but they know little about their divinity. Even today, most people no longer know about their origin; they do not know where they go after the death of their body and they do not know the law of sowing and reaping, the principle that what a person sows, that is, sends, is what he receives, what he reaps.

The emerging human beings limited themselves to their own primitive thought world, which they considered to be something great, that is, god-like; for their domination and power over their neighbor showed itself more and more. From this, they concluded that they were gods. Their conceptions and terms became forms that they still call reality today.

Let us look at the present time. The majority of people are satisfied with their primitive thought world, with the confining consciousness of "mine" and "me." Many strive to climb the ladder of success and many use their elbows unscrupulously, in order to climb the rungs of the ladder as fast as possible, to gain power, prestige and wealth. This is their reality; these are their self-made, tangible forms and their norms.

Since the cup is now full, that is, the energy of God on loan is mostly used up and thus reversed, the negative energy can be shifted around for a limited time only. The causal event, in which the wheel of reincarnation turns, cannot continue as before. The time is near when this wheel will gradually come to a stop. This then means for every individual to either accept Christ and fulfill the laws of life or to suffer death and remain spiritually dead for eons as a soul in the purification planes, without the recognition that divinity dwells in the depths of its soul.

But God, our all-wise, eternal Father is near His children even in the darkness of an existence far from God. The incorruptible divine energy, which is also the maintaining energy of the reversed - now negative - energy, and which cannot be transformed down, remains in every component of matter and in every component of the purification planes. This means that sooner or later the souls or the human beings will again reverse the transformed-down energy from negative to positive with Christ, their Redeemer, who is the maintaining energy, in order to bring it into the eternal law. This is an irrevocable law.

And so, we now stand before the "either - or." Either we, as human beings, transform and transfer back into the eternal law the part of energy that was reversed by us - or we do this by suffering as souls in the spheres of purification. Either we save ourselves and our planet by changing ourselves - or we destroy our world and enter spiritual death. With "world," I mean the human establishments, everything that man has created with his conceptions and terms.

The divine energy on loan has to be returned. This is in the law of leading-back, which Jesus of Nazareth, the Christ of God, accepted through His Redeemer-deed. Because God *is* and remains unchangeable, the pure, incorruptible energy in all the building blocks of infinity, also in matter, is the pulling and pushing power for the work of completion.

The will of the Fall-beings then and today: to create people according to their own image

Let's go back again to the emerging human beings, because the event of the Fall can especially help one understand the present time.

The wish-programs of the emerging human beings of that time were to create bodies. Through the intensification of their wish-thoughts, reproductive organs gradually were formed in the developing human beings. When this restructuring had been accomplished in the further course of condensation, they became aware that they could no longer attract rebellious beings from other Fall-worlds which corresponded to their consciousness and which they could dominate and control. And so, it was no longer possible, as before, to directly call beings from other worlds to them, that is, to get them here, as it were, so that they could live with them, on earth, and serve their purposes. They were now dependent on reproductive organs, with which they procreated shells and into which other beings, that is, souls, could implant themselves.

So let's look at our world. What do many scientists want? Through gene manipulation, they want to create human beings because procreation alone has become too uncertain for them, since the genetic material is under the effects of the causes produced by mankind, and the chances are becoming ever smaller that healthy and robust bodies can be procreated that are capable of living on a polluted earth and in a destroyed atmosphere.

Science realizes that the old is no longer useful and so something new has to come about. Through gene manipulation, one thinks it is possible to create a new earth, new people and a new "heaven" - that is, new repository stars.

The first steps in this direction have already been initiated; they are seen in the experiments that are already done with animals, plants and food, because the plants and animals, too, with their genetic material, are no longer able to exist unchanged under the conditions of a changed cosmic radiation.

Today's man is not much further along than pre-historic man, the emerging human being. Many are still not aware today that what they are able to procreate is just a shell that corresponds to their predispositions, that is, their genetic material.

Many people were and are of the opinion that man either has no soul or that the body itself is the soul. The causal computer stores all these thoughts and ideas. From there, these inputs radiate back to the people who are receptive for this. They receive either through telepathy from souls or from groups of souls, or they retrieve from the cosmic computer system their own inputs and think, even admire, how ingenious they are.

The consciousness of developing human beings was no longer sufficient to be able to recognize that in the fine-material realms were many beings from the Fall which, like them, wanted to become human beings, but could no longer reach the process of condensation, because sexual and reproductive organs were already forming in the emerging human beings.

The Fall-beings, which could no longer take the direct path of condensation, instead being dependent on receiving an opportunity to incarnate, made contact with the developing human beings, influencing and urging them to procreate bodies - which inhabitants of earth at that time thought to be creations. To procreate a body into which a being could incarnate was something new for them. And so, they acted unknowingly.

We have known about the ability to procreate as far as we can think back. However, in the beginning this was unknown to the emerging human beings. The names Adam and Eve stand for the first human beings who were capable of procreation.

For the so-called completely developed human beings, it is perfectly normal to procreate a child. But for many people it seems abnormal to think that a soul can be attracted from those regions of the beyond that correspond to the state of consciousness of both parents. Whether we are aware of it or not, through the act of procreation, the one procreating and the one conceiving call, so to speak, a soul which corresponds to the vibration of both of them, of the procreator and receiver.

Let's look at the present time. What does man want? Many scientists want to create genetically altered human beings, who correspond to their will, namely, who think and act in the way that those in power and their power-monopolies prescribe - people according to their image. We see that the emerging human being and the completely developed human being are still similar to each other - even though time after time - we call them light-cycle after light-cycle - lie between them.

Because of sin, the consciousness of the first human beings became narrower and narrower and work on a still barren earth became harder and harder. The nervous system that was still developing in the physical body was tense, so that with the physical act they felt the first feelings of lust and well-being, since it brought them a brief period of relaxation.

When the sexual union produced the first physical bodies, which were born according to the moon cycles, the first human beings stood there in astonishment. They could not comprehend what kind of creature was given to them here. They saw a small human being, that is, a newborn baby, and didn't quite know what to do with it.

The first people oriented themselves according to the course of the stars. They consulted the stars and thought the stars would help them. But it was not the stars which helped the first people in word and deed, but the Fall-beings, that is, the souls, which dwelt on the various stars and planets. These souls emitted and the people received. In this way, telepathy developed, the sending and receiving between this side of life and the beyond. It still takes place today in a similar way: To wherever a person emits, from there he receives.

Via the principle of sending and receiving, the first human beings received telepathic vibrations. These were impulses from souls, that is, from Fall-beings, which gradually explained to them what this small body, the new human being, was all about: That it needed food, that it needed movement and above all that a being from the Fall-realms was and is in this body, whose spirit-body is folded in - we could also say encapsulated - and which, in the course of growing and maturing as a human being, will unfold as far as the spiritual consciousness can develop.

In order to better understand this being folded into itself, we have to be aware that the spiritual body consists of spiritual particles, which in their arrangement and form can be compared to honeycombs. When a soul incarnates, these particles fold together. With the first cry of the child, the soul is linked with the physical body. The soul then unfolds in the person according to how the child grows and matures. The degree of unfoldment of the soul depends on the consciousness of the soul and on the genetic components which are active in the person.

Via telepathy from the Fall-realms, the first human beings also received knowledge about reincarnation, about the slipping into and out of the flesh. Today, we now call the burdened being, which incarnates and reincarnates, simply the soul.

The cycle designated for the turning-back of mankind is coming to an end. After the collapse of the Fall-structure, the assimilation of all condensed matter into the pure Being

God gave His children free will and though this the opportunity to carry out their plan as they wished. But God reserved the right to take back the energies loaned when their plan would fail.

God is unchangeable and is present in all things. God *is*, and God cannot be changed or persuaded. Even though the Eternal knew that this Fall-plan - of wanting to be like God, yes, even to surpass God - could not and cannot be carried out, because the Absolute cannot be shaken and conquered, He, the great Spirit, granted His children this plan. For only by way of self-recognition, will they find their way back to their origin, to the true Being. The free will is decisive.

God granted and grants the Fall-children the opportunity to recognize themselves in their own thoughts, in their self-made law, in their conceptions and terms, in their human self that took on form and is far from God. This is why the way back to God for human beings is: Recognize yourself, follow the path of remorse, of asking for forgiveness, of forgiving, of making amends - and do not commit what you know to be sinful.

Through self-recognition, through earnest remorse and by clearing up the causes, that is, the sinfulness, the souls and human beings find access to God again, through the positive divine principle of giving and receiving. He, the All-wise, knew that through self-recognition His children would awaken to the awareness of the filiation in God, because they remained and remain divine deep in their soul through His omnipresence.

For turning back and returning to the divine Being, God gave man a length of time that is for us unimaginably long, perhaps billions of years. Let us not calculate in years, but in cycles within the Fall-event, for all of infinity runs in rhythmic cycles. The spiritual law of evolution, the becoming and growing to full maturity, which is the perfection of life, is effective in these movements of infinity. Full maturity means that the being which is divine again has again unfolded all the powers of infinity in itself. On matter, which is a part of the Fall-realms, and within the brevity of years, the soul in man can and should unfold again all the powers of infinity, its divine heritage, which is covered over by sin.

Man's life course also runs in cycles. His living and dying phases - also called "lifespan and deathspan" - run in cycles, until death finally comes. Then the person should have cleansed his soul for the most part. The Fall-event, too, runs in pre-set cycles from its beginning to its end. This sequence is called the actualization span and the fulfillment span of mankind, within which every one is given the opportunity to turn back.

The Fall is coming to an end according to pre-set cycles. A cycle, a certain length of time, is also designated for leading the soul of a person back. When this cycle ends, leading the person back is no longer possible either. This then means for the burdened human being that it dies and then, as a soul, enters the cycle of being led back, which is given in those Fall-realms that are no longer matter, that is, that are finer regions. But there, the quick turning back through probation does not exist. There, one must expiate. And this means to suffer and endure all that which the human being inflicted on others.

Whether mankind turns back or not - at the end of this actualization and fulfillment span, at the end of the last cycle, the entire structure of the Fall on this earth will gradually collapse. It will be transformed by the stars and planets, which bear in themselves the principle of transformation, from coarse materiality to finer matter. Through this principle of transformation, density will be brought into higher vibration, that is, it will be refined. At the same time, this process of transformation also takes place in the material universe. This lawful transformation, too, happens in cycles.

The transformation will take place cyclically, that is, in phases, until the transformed-down energy of God that is on loan is again highest vibrating eternal power, which then merges into the eternal law, whence it was given.

This cyclical process of evolution happens in all purification planes, including the earth. When this has been accomplished, the assimilation into the sublime consciousness of God has been completed. The material macrocosm is now in this time of radical change to the New Era - in the last mighty cycle of matter.

Jesus, the Christ of God, accomplished something unimaginably great for souls and men. His unswerving steadfastness brought about the turning-point in the Fall-event

The leading-back of human souls and the assimilation into the eternal Being began already nearly two thousand years ago. This time was initiated with the coming of Jesus, the Christ. And so, the last mighty cycle of density already lies in the words "It is finished."

Jesus, the Christ, came to mankind. He taught the Ten Commandments and brought the Sermon on the Mount, which are excerpts from the cosmic law.

Through the "It is finished" of the Son of God on the cross, something powerful took place in all souls. The Son of God loaned a part of His divine heritage to all souls as support and as motive power, in order to again establish a connection with the power of God, the energy of the Father, the eternal law, so that human beings are once again conscious sons and daughters of God.

This supporting power, the Redeemer-spark, was necessary, because the souls were on the verge of their dissolution, since souls and men had used up the energy of God more and more. The Redeemer-spark prevented the souls from coming to or even going beyond this point of tipping over. The transforming down of the spirit body - via the kingdoms of the animals, plants and minerals - right down to dissolution, can no longer take place.

The dissolution of all forms, even of all universes - was the wish and objective of the Fall-beings. So this plan will not be fulfilled. Even though mankind is using up God's energy more and more - thus completely filling the memory bank of the two macrocosms, the purification planes and matter, with negative energy - the Redeemer-light remains the supporting and guiding power into the Father's house. The Redeemer-light cannot be reversed, that is, transformed down.

What happens when the memory bank can no longer absorb any more negative energy? The full memory bank, which contains the causes of mankind and of the souls in the purification planes, empties more and more. This means that the causes are coming toward mankind faster and faster. They no longer come in phases, in waves, but in many cases, they come all at once and to their full extent. Therefore, a cause no longer comes to effect in segments, but often concentratedly, in its full effect.

And so, we learn that Jesus, the Christ of God, accomplished the unimaginably great for all souls and men. As a human being, He faced the opposing forces. He, the great Spirit in the human being, wrestled with the forces of the darkness and through His steadfastness showed the adversary that God is invincible. Jesus is the example for all people.

If Jesus, the Christ of God, had wavered, then God's opponent would have conquered the Son of God. His part-power of the primordial power would then have gone into the demonic realm. Then the part-power of the primordial power would have become a negative power in the service of the demons and the prince of darkness would have gained another energy-potential, with which he could have brought about what was and still is in his plan: the dissolution of the Kingdom of God and of all spiritual forms of life.

The Eternal, the all-wise One, knew that His Son would be victorious. On the cross, Jesus spoke the mighty words of transformation "It is finished." Through His Redeemer-deed, the entire Fall, the macrocosm of the purification planes, the macrocosm of matter and everything that lives in these two star-worlds, will now be led back. With this, the transformation and the leading-back to the eternal Being are then completed.

And so, mankind now lives in the last mighty cycle of transformation. The sinful world passes away; the Kingdom of God will emerge more and more - just as the prophets of the Old Covenant already prophesied. It is not the earth that will be destroyed, but this world. All its establishments will pass away, and many people who do not bear the sign of love on their foreheads will perish with their world.

The part-power of the primordial power, the Redeemer-power, brought about the turning point in the Fall-event. With this, the demons suffered their first great defeat. They could not conquer the Son of God.

The human being – a planet in the All. Coming and going – Dying and becoming

As long as a person lives in the law of sowing and reaping, he is a marked one and thus programmed. He can be compared to a computer, which has stored in itself everything that went out and still goes out from him, for it is what entered and enters him again.

Since each one is the portrayal of his feeling, thinking, wanting and doing, the chromosomes of the person, the hereditary predispositions, are imprinted accordingly. This imprinting is the physical heritage of the person which lies in his genes. Every person finds himself in his genes and in the cosmos. And so, each one of us is his own memory bank and each one marks himself and is thus the marked one.

We can be sure that God, the eternal law, His great cosmic bookkeeping, the mighty cosmic computer, is exact and just. Nothing is ever lost; everything is registered.

Every human being and every soul can be compared with a planet. Both have their orbits, the person as well as the soul, according to their characteristics and attributes. In the Spirit of God, the law of gravitation says: like attracts like - in matter, it is the attraction of the masses. Through this spiritual law of communication, the human being, the incarnated soul, the planet, moves into its orbit accordingly.

When the body dies, the soul leaves its shell, the physical body, behind. This process of dying and the decay of the physical body can be compared with those stars that burn out and go into the vortex of the so-called "black holes." These appear more and more often in the universe, because more and more stars burn out. The black holes are the graves in the All, where burnt out stars are transformed. They either become matter again or they are brought into a higher aggregate state.

When we speak of matter, then we have to be aware that it does not have eternal life. However, the spiritual body - in a shadowed state, the soul - has eternal life. The spiritual body, that is, the soul, cannot burn out and cannot decay - nor can the spiritual substance deep within the material star, which we could call its soul. Only the density of matter burns out and decays. It is transformed "in the graves of the All." In the same way, the human body is transformed back into the elements from which it was formed. It is different with the soul; it enters its journey either in higher spheres of life, or it stays in the wheel of reincarnation, in the alternation of slipping in and out of the flesh, until it has largely put aside its burdens, its sins. This coming and going continues, until an incarnation is no longer possible.

Let it be said once more: We learn about the development of souls and planets. Planets die and are attracted by the "graves in the All," the black holes. Out of these, either the birth of new stars and planets takes place, or the mass is brought into a higher aggregate state and, by way of further refinement, very gradually attains assimilation into the All-computer, the high law of perfect life, the eternal Being.

The soul has the opportunity to attain assimilation into the eternal Being, by giving up its sinfulness, that is, its burdens, in the purification spheres. However, it can also incarnate again, that is, it can become a new planet in the earthly garment, a human being, which again moves into its orbit on earth.

The same principle is valid for the entire material macrocosm: the entrance and exit. It is the coming and going; these are the changes through the various aggregate states. This cosmic event will continue until the actualization and fulfillment spans come to an end. Through the radiation of the causal computer, the soul is led to a decision: either incarnation - as long as the possibility of incarnation still exists - or expiation in the soul realms.

Only that comes toward the soul in the spheres of purification and to the soul in a human being, which this soul has entered into the causal computer during a former life in the physical body. When a soul goes into incarnation, then, as already described, it develops a new earthly body. In the same way as the embryo develops in the body of the mother, the registration of this developing body is entered into the material computer system.

When many souls incarnate, then it is possible that new material stars are born again from the black holes - computer components for the registration of the many procreated human bodies. When the embryos develop in the mothers' bodies, then the repository planets which develop from the supernovas emerge from the black holes. They then move into their orbits in the material cosmos in accordance with what is stored in them. Their storage potential corresponds to the radiation potential of the many human bodies, which were born and in which corresponding souls incarnated with the same and similar predispositions, contained in the genes of the physical body.

The nature kingdoms with their species of plants and animals are subject to the same principle as the human beings - dying and becoming. And let us bring to mind again that all occurrences of human beings and souls, as well as those of the nature kingdoms and the mineral kingdoms, are registered in the cosmos.

When a great many animals and plants die out, then it is possible that planets again burn out and are attracted by the mass graves, the black holes. This also holds true for the changes in the mineral kingdoms. Every change and every process of dying, as well as the gradual decay of the physical body of the animals and plants, is directed by the computer system.

And so, the world of the stars is not only the bookkeeping of God for the Fall-worlds, but also the eye of God; for the stars and planets precisely follow every single course of development on matter. If a dead body is cremated or burned - this holds true for animals and plants, as well - then this process also takes place accordingly in the material cosmos and in the cosmos of the purification planes. What is left over radiates, that is, it sends and receives at the same time. As a result of this, what is left over - for example, the ashes and its subsequent decay, as well as everything that gradually decays on and in the earth - is also connected with the material cosmos.

The eye of the All - the planets of the Fall-worlds - observes and registers the least movement in and on the earth as well as in the soul realms. When many species of animals and plants die out, whose spiritual potential no longer appears on earth as an animal or a plant, then the radiation-potential of those stars, in which these species of animal or plant were stored and which were absorbed by the black holes, gradually become assimilated into the eternal Being.

I repeat: Every change is registered in the cosmos, and what is registered radiates back accordingly. Through this, everything is in communication with everything. Every stone that is crushed, ground up or taken to another place for a suitable use - all these movements and occurrences are registered in the material macrocosm.

Through the principle of sending and receiving, through the registration and the return radiation, an absolute communication is guaranteed, and thus an absolute bookkeeping. This mighty gravitational network, that is, communication network, can only be partially comprehended by us as human beings.

The human being is controlled by his own registration. Hereditary predispositions are magnets. Abortion – A sin against life

Everything is consciousness. Just as we think, so do we live. Our genes, too, are consciousness. For the most part, they are made up of what the person feels, senses, thinks, speaks and does. In the course of time, feelings, thoughts, words and deeds that return again and again form building blocks, which, as a general term, we call hereditary predispositions. This is our human heritage; this is what we surround ourselves with, with which we think, speak and act.

Our genetic material is thus recorded in the computer system of the stars. Through the principle of sending and receiving, every building block, every hereditary predisposition, is a corresponding magnet. Our human genetic makeup overlays the divine heritage which consists of the principles of equality, freedom, unity and brotherliness.

The fallout of our human inputs, that is, of what is in our genes - our physical heritage - then also has its effect in the temporal. In this world, we create for ourselves what already lies in our genetic material. We are an artisan, a teacher, a theologian, a scientist, a physician. We want to realize in the world what our hereditary predispositions radiate out. And so, we can say that it is no coincidence when, for instance, scientists or researchers or physicians or artisans appear again and again in a particular ancestral line. These may always be the same souls which also meet one another in the earthly garment, in order to expiate what they have together inflicted upon themselves as physical genetic material, that is, as humanness.

No matter which elements of human consciousness of feelings, thoughts, words and wanting are linked together to form our human genetic material, it has to be cleared up or expiated and transformed - from the human, the sinful, to the divine, the unburdened. The negative energy has to become positive energy again. What was loaned has to be brought back. And so, the earth is a place of expiation and probation for all people, no matter which rank, title, name or profession they may have.

The expiation - by which clearing things up has to take place - leads to the transformation of the negative to the positive in soul and person and, at the same time, to a rearrangement in the world of the stars. Through the principle of "like attracts like," people come together who have created causes with each other, in order to be able to pay these off together. The same principle holds true in the soul realms for the souls.

And so, it is possible that into a human child is born that soul, which in a former existence was perhaps a brother or sister of its present earthly mother, or the mother or the father of the present mother or of the present father, or a former relative - depending on which causes there are that should be cleared up together during this life on earth. The whole family meets again, but in different garments and in different roles.

That which is not atoned has to be atoned. And so, if, in accordance with the law of sowing and reaping, there are karmic knots - for example, a family karma that should be cleared up during this life on earth - the former family comes together again in a new earthly existence, but as different components.

It is not by chance that we were born into our family, that we encounter this or that person, that we are placed in this job and not another. Why we go here and there today, why we move harmoniously or hectically today, why we harbor this or that feeling or sensation, or what we think, speak and do today, wherever we go, wherever we drive - all this has its reason and wants to tell us something. For every stirring, every movement, every feeling, every sensation, every thought, every word and every action is registered and comes back to the programmer, the sender, by way of return radiation.

And so, it is of no use for us to want to externally change the conditions of our life on earth. All resistance against our fate is fruitless. Only when we recognize and clear things up, that is, when we change, will our life also change as a result.

We are controlled by our own causal registration and only by way of this are we brought together with other people again - when we have causes to clear up with them.

And so, every time we are brought together with someone, it means something. Some are brought together to clear up their causes with each other; others are brought together in order to fulfill a divine mission in accordance with the eternal law, if this mission is recorded in the divine worlds. The scale of our feeling, thinking, speaking and wanting tells us what brings us together.

Many people can be kept blind by the opponent of God, because they do not think about their life, which consists of their feeling, thinking, speaking and wanting. They do what others decide - with the reasoning that the others know better. But God gave every human being a mind, so that he can understand and recognize things. The one who wants to figure out what is good or evil can measure his thinking and doing against the Ten Commandments and the Sermon on the Mount of Jesus; for these principles are excerpts from the Absolute Law, God.

Let it be said once more: Many people do not think about their life, where it comes from and who or what life is. One basic rule of ethics for mankind says: Save life and protect life. This principle should also hold true for the embryo. But many abort a growing child unscrupulously and do not know that in doing so they are driving away a soul with which they should have cleared up some things in this earthly existence. According to the eternal laws, abortion comes under the fifth principle of the Ten Commandments: You shall not kill.

Therefore, an abortion - at whatever stage - is a grave sin, a sin against life. The present legislation of many countries, that one may abort depending on the situation, is a demonic ruling. Every sin has to be paid off. What is not paid off, that is, what is not cleared up, has to be cleared up one day. That which is not cleared up now, in this life, has to be atoned for and cleared up in the purification planes or in future incarnations.

The one who aborts a growing child has committed murder and thus has burdened himself accordingly. The soul, which wanted to come as a human being to one or more people, in order to clear up some things with them, that is, to expiate, now has to keep these causes in its soul body. All the people who agreed to the abortion - the politician who voted for the legislation, the one who carried out the abortion, the one who had the abortion or who motivated the latter to do so - are all a part of this sinful event.

In this way, too, a group karma can develop. It means that these people who have created causes together will be brought together again, either in the spheres of purification as souls or again as human beings. The law of karma knows the way and brings together those people who should pay off and expiate together what they once caused together.

The significance of an incarnation for a soul – The effort and trouble before and after birth

What cannot be seen on matter is dismissed by many people as trivial, and yet before an incarnation or before the procreation of a child, cosmic processes take place that man cannot grasp because his senses are oriented toward the visible and seldom register what happens behind the facade of the human ego - which is already in movement before the person thinks or before, for example, a child is procreated.

And so, let us become aware that when a soul incarnates, and before the procreation of its body, has already dealt with many things: all the preparations in the beyond, its alignment with its path to incarnation, the waiting until procreation - that is, that a magnet is created - and then the course of development via the life path, via certain constellations of the stars, to earth, to incarnation.

When the soul has incarnated, then again begins - perhaps for the tenth, the twentieth, the hundredth, the thousandth time - the action of setting into motion the human body that it has taken on. The same thing happens again and again. Again and again, the soul has to prepare the shell of its body, the small vehicle, for this earth.

It has to learn to master its human body. This happens very gradually and with many setbacks. It has to newly program its body, starting with the brain. It thus needs - perhaps for the hundredth time - life programs again, in order to be able to exist on this earth as a human being. For perhaps the hundredth, the two-hundredth, time, it has to rely on the parents, the grandparents, the relatives, who help it enter the basic programs into the new brain: speaking, touching, sitting, walking and much more. Later - for perhaps the two-hundredth time - the environment again has an influence on the child. With its pictures, opinions and conditions, the environment moves the soul of the child into another era, in order to now store what the new person needs in this era to live on the earth.

If the parents pay enough attention to their child, they see with how much effort the soul of their child learns to master its vehicle, the physical body, and how long the human being needs until the first programs for this new life on earth take effect - even the first words of the child, most often "mommy" or "daddy," are programmed. Letter by letter, sound by sound, the words are built into the brain. The first signs that a program is forming are often only individual sounds, from which words are gradually formulated. It is often only "da" or "ma." It takes a long time until the child can pronounce the words.

When the child has developed some programs, for instance, "daddy" or "mommy," then these programs, these words, have also become a picture in the child. In the same way that the word - that is, the picture - forms in the brain of the person, it is also registered in the material stars. The child is then in communication with these programs and continues to build on them and create further programs for its earthly existence. Even the child's babbling indicates that pictorial programs are developing in him, which at the same time are forming in the stars. The babbling also indicates a registration in the stars, because there is no movement and no sound without communication.

And so, we can see what it means for a soul to incarnate, what effort and trouble is necessary - even before procreation, then during the development of the child in the womb and then from birth on. And all this is simply swept away with an operation or a few pills!

The soul has to give consideration to the genetic material of its new body, in order to activate those genetic predispositions - which correspond to the energy potential that it brought with it - as far as the person needs them while going through the different stages of maturity. Some components of the genes of the mother and father are also contained in the genetic material of the child, because the soul of the child was attracted by the parents via like-vibrating programs, in order to clear up in the family what connects them with one another.

The soul in its new earthly life also has to activate the five senses of its body, in order to be able to steer the vehicle, the human being, in the right way. By activating the five senses, which, in turn, takes place by way of the genetic material, further pictorial programs emerge which will be taken in by the child's genes as new programs and by the soul as radiation potential. The soul puts up with the many arduous difficulties of learning, of standing up, of sitting, of standing and walking in the earthly body.

The soul has to develop anew what the small child wants, where it wants to walk to and the like. This is why it is decisive for the small child what the mother, the father, the grandparents, the relatives and acquaintances say and what they put into their words. The sensitive soul in the new earthly body is very alert and grasps the world of thoughts of the people who surround the child.

The many impressions - everything that the child faces - even the pictures of the thoughts of the father, mother, grandparents, relatives and so on are registered by the soul. In many cases, what it perceives goes to be stored in the brain of the small child, in its soul and in the stars. The first life pictures, then result from this, the first impressions of the soul in its new body.

And so, the mother, father, grandparents and relatives place the pictures of what they have learned into the world of the child. What the words "father," "mother," "sun," "flower" and so forth mean to the parents, the grandparents and relatives, that is, how they feel about these terms, which the grown-ups have made into a picture for themselves, it is according to this that the pictures and their meanings also emerge in the brain of the child, in the soul and in the stars.

With the words that the child has learned - "father" or "papa," "mother" or "mama," "grandma," "grandpa," "aunt," "uncle" - the child makes conscious contact with its father, its mother, its grandparents, its relatives and acquaintances. The child sees its parents as they present themselves to it - it takes in words and pictures, whereby the behavior of the people who surround the child are in the pictures. From this, gradually emerge the first programs and in the course of time more programs. And so, very gradually the brain, the soul and the stars are programmed.

Programs determine the life of a person. Creating further programs as sending and receiving stations

Because the statement about a language of pictures is important, I want to repeat once more: The child which is starting to talk, sees the father, the mother, the grandparents and the relatives - the people who presently determine its life - according to their radiation, and not as they see themselves or as they would like to be seen. In its body, the alert soul is focused on recognizing, learning and programming, because its first task in its earthly life is to learn to master its physical body.

The brain of the small child absorbs things according to the genetic material of the new physical body and according to the behavior of the adults. For instance, the child will perceive the sun, the flower, the stone, the animal, the person, completely differently than, for example, its parents, grandparents or, in the course of its life, all other people, with whom the growing person has contact.

The person perceives his surroundings in accordance with the radiation he has brought with him which is reflected in his genes and with what was programmed into him by his parents, grandparents, relatives and acquaintances. As a result of this, every person sees every other person differently. He will also perceive his environment, that is, everything that surrounds him, differently than his fellow men. Everyone will also define and describe differently what comes toward him. Every person and the soul that dwells in him radiate out what they have taken in as programs.

The genes and the entire person are marked by the principle of sending and receiving. The first cry of the newborn already contains the first information about the small person whose soul now finds itself in this world, on this earth. It is its first sending in the earthly garment. The information that is contained in the first cry and is expressed in the first movement of the body is already data, which is immediately stored in the computer, in the stars.

We recognize the accuracy of the bookkeeping of God. Everything - every movement, every stirring, every program that is forming, including the growth of the child - is perceived and registered down to the last detail by the great memory bank of the bookkeeping of God. The new citizen of the earth is already in communication with these, his own inputs.

The person reacts in accordance with his programs which form his sending and receiving station, and from where the impulses of the day go out. This is why every person behaves differently when faced with the various things of life. For instance, the senses of sight and hearing work closely together. And so, the person acts in his life according to the programs that he has created, that is, taken on, with his senses of sight and hearing.

The same is true for the senses of smell, taste and touch. What the person has seen, heard, smelled, tasted and touched became his programs, which are also stored in the computer system of the stars.

The countdown of life starts running with the first cry of the child. These processes take place in the cosmos and in the person. This is the way the person behaves - this is his life. The entire range of his feeling, sensing, thinking, speaking and acting, of his five senses and of his wanting and wishing are programs of reaction, that is, inputs in his brain and partly in his soul, too. And so, the person can act and react only on the basis of his own inputs. Nothing beyond that is possible, unless he enters the corresponding programs beforehand, which again happens via his five senses.

And so, every person is a computer. For example, the person hears conversations, and even though it may be only a part of a conversation, he thinks about it, because he has stored the words, the terms, that is, the language. For a person, a word is a term. He has stored this one word in him by learning the language. This one word says one thing to this person and something else to another, according to what the person has placed into this word as a picture and as what he wants. When he now hears this word, then this picture and what he wants comes up in him. The picture and what he wants are made up, in turn, of different thought combinations. From these, he makes himself a new picture - according to the energy of the day, according to the person from whose mouth he heard the words, according to his surroundings and, not least, according to his momentary physical situation. Further programs then emerge from these often unrelated words, that is, terms. Just as they emerge, they go into the consciousness and the subconscious, and some time later into the soul and then into the computer system of the macrocosms that were conditioned by the Fall.

The person expresses what he himself has stored. Because his inputs are entered at the same time into the cosmic computer systems, in this sense he is also the microcosm in the macrocosm.

With our inputs, we continually call up information from this information source of the macrocosms - mostly what we ourselves have entered into them. But beyond that, we can try to contact other sources of information, when these are similar to our sending potential. What we receive from these sources we perceive, in part in the consciousness; we think about it and, in this way, too, expand our programs, our sending and receiving potential.

Everything is contained in all things. Sowing and reaping can be seen in the components of the body.

Stones, plants and animals, too, are in communication with the three macrocosms. Like people, the nature kingdoms are condensed energies and thus also connected with human beings. For this reason, the animals, for example, absorb from human beings what is good and not so good, including what the latter inflict on them. The actions of people which the animals perceive do not burden them, because animals do not sin.

Stones, plants and animals on the earth are spiritual forms of life which are enveloped with a material garment, in order to serve us human beings. In the great spiritual event of evolution, they are degrees of consciousness that have taken on form. The further spiritual development of a life form takes place in the spiritual planes of development of the eternal Being.

In stones, plants and animals, the communication with the Creator-Spirit consists of divine perception. The individual life form, which is in the process of evolution in order to mature into a perfect spirit being, receives impulses from the Creator-Spirit for its spiritual evolution and maturity, in accordance with its state of development. The perfect spirit body develops from these evolutionary steps. Just as the spiritual body develops and unfolds in the eternal Being, in a similar way the development process of an embryo takes place in the womb of the mother.

The full maturity of a spirit being consists in the fact that its perfect spiritual body is compressed, eternal divine law, its divine heritage.

The pure, perfect divine beings possess infinity as a whole, compressed in and around themselves. In the spiritual nature kingdoms, the divine heritage builds up in an evolutionary process, until everything is active in all things - the perfect spiritual body, the divine heritage.

In accordance with the eternal divine principle, everything is contained in all things. Just as it is in the eternal Being - in a similar way it also takes place on earth. Our human heritage builds up through our feeling, thinking, speaking and wanting. It is reflected in and on our body, as well as in our blood and in the functioning of our organs. The actions and reactions in and on our body are controlled by our brain, which contains the programs of our world of feelings, thoughts and senses.

The spiritual body consists of spiritual particles. The whole of infinity is contained in each of these particles. It is similar with human beings. In every cell and in every drop of blood, is contained the entire picture of the person, his entire sending and receiving potential, everything that is atoned or unatoned, that is, cleared up or not cleared up.

We recognize that sowing and reaping, too, can be seen in all the components of our body.

And so, it can be said that one drop of blood, for instance, contains what we have entered into the memory bank of the stars - from the first cry of the newborn until the last breath of the person. One drop of blood already tells who we are. One drop of blood also lets one see if causes from the cosmos are active or will become active or if effects have been cleared up. And so, a drop of blood shows the radiation picture of the soul and of the person.

When we look into the operations of the material cosmos that are partly known to us, then the galaxies, the milky ways, among other things, open up to us. We could call these the lymph and blood pathways of the cosmos. The processes of the lymph and of the blood of every single person is stored in them. They influence the person through the principle of sending and receiving.

We can compare the material cosmos with a huge, cosmic human being and every human being, in turn, with the cosmos; this is why man is the microcosm in the macrocosm.

All three, the fine-material macrocosms and the coarse-material macrocosm, are built according to the one principle: Everything is contained in all things - the smallest in the large and the large in the smallest.

Nothing happens by chance. Bringing people together for the purpose of clearing things up

The human being emerged through crystallization by way of Fall-thoughts and so he is modified ether. The soul begins to again become pure divine substance by clearing up the density, the burdens, which often takes places over incarnations.

The law of cause and effect, the causal law, is nothing new to the one who knows about reincarnation. He is aware that everything negative has to be cleared up, if not in incarnations, then in the spheres of purification, in the macrocosm of the purification planes. From the age when he can tell the difference between good and bad, the young person himself is responsible for his life. He cannot make his fellow man responsible for his fate, because his harvest is also his seed.

We will not progress in our life if we blame what is meant for us and what happens to us, on our parents, grandparents, relatives, friends, our colleagues at work or our husband or wife or partner. Based on the principle of sending and receiving and the accuracy of the bookkeeping of

God, that anything happens by chance is not possible. And so, as we have already explained, it is not by chance that these circumstances of life mark our existence, that we have learned precisely this profession and that we work with these colleagues. It is also not by chance that we have these friends and not others, just as it is no coincidence that we found our way to our husband or wife or partner.

Again and again, the law of cause and effect leads people together who should clear something up with each other. And so, disputes should tell us what is not in order with our own self. Strife and trouble with our partner tell us which part we have in it, what *we* should recognize and clear up.

It is also not by chance that among many people, we find one person pleasant and are happy to see him. This tells us that we have a positive connection, a connection of the soul, with him. In the same way, it is no coincidence that among many people, we find one person unpleasant, that spontaneously we dislike this or that about him, so that we get irritated by this even though we don't know him.

It is not even by chance that an animal attacks us, that a dog barks at us, and we are *irritated* by it, or that we trip over a stone.

It is not a coincidence that our eyes stick to a particular object or to a person. The thoughts that we have about it are significant for us. They tell us who we are. Also the corresponding sensations, feelings and thoughts that are awakened by what we hear, smell, taste and touch tell us who we are.

The atmospheric chronicle is full. The debit account of mankind

Our life will become interesting when we are willing to look at ourselves. Only then will we become aware of who we still are as a person and what we have entered into the stars, into the causal computer.

If we feel well today, then this, too, is a radiation from the stars. When we feel indisposed today, then it is not our neighbor who is to blame - we ourselves have at some time sent out what is not good, the indisposition, and now we receive it again. It wants to stimulate us to think about our sensations, feelings and thoughts, so that we may recognize ourselves and clear up our humanness. In this way, we reverse what is negative and gain positive energy.

Not one iota is lost in the All. For instance, each hair on the head of every person is numbered. Everything is registered. The sparrow, too, that falls from the roof of the house is recorded in the computer system and can fall from the roof only because its time on this earth has run out and the stars have introduced and carried out the death of the sparrow.

There is a spiritual layer in the atmosphere. It is called the chronicle of mankind by those who are spiritually knowing. It contains the history of all the generations of mankind. Everything that human beings have ever sensed, felt, thought, spoken and done, which should be paid off and cleared up on the earth, remains in this atmospheric chronicle.

When a person dies who, for example, took part in the fate of a nation, or in the fate of several people, then these causes, these processes of human interconnections, remain in this spiritual layer. These causes are also registered in the causal computer. Only the life programs that the soul needed as a human being in order to live on the earth, to express itself and to find its way around are erased after the incarnation has run its course. They are the programs of language, the programs of education, the programs of eating, of communication, and so forth.

The laws of God that were given to mankind by Jesus of Nazareth, by the prophets and enlightened ones are also in the atmospheric chronicle. Because these given divine laws were heard by mankind, because many of them were recorded in books, but not yet fulfilled, they remained in the atmospheric chronicle and are also registered in the causal computer. These spurned gifts of God, whose actualization would have led man to a happy, contented and healthy life and to unity with the earth, are the debit account of mankind. Every individual - whether he is presently a human being or a soul - is bound to this debt of the peoples, if he contributed to the defilement of the earth and to harming people and the nature kingdoms.

The one who, for example, calls himself Christian and does not live in a Christian manner is part of this collective debt. The guilt of Christianity consists of sinning despite knowing better, because Christians know the Ten Commandments and the Sermon on the Mount. Among other things, the debit account consists of causing wars, devastation, poisoning the earth and the waters, of the responsibility for the suffering of the animals and plants, and not lastly for the destruction of the earth's ozone layer.

In this spiritual layer, the atmospheric chronicle, are also stored the experiments and undertakings of former scientists who, as we have already said, want to continue their human achievements in this world using various ways and means. The theological doctrines and opinions are also stored, and will continue to be stored until they are eliminated in this world, that is, until they are erased, transformed. The causes that are not paid off, including those which the statesmen of the different generations have set, remain and again affect the world and those people who were and are a part of them.

As long as that which the various memory banks contain is not paid off and thus transformed - from negative, that is, transformed-down energy to positive energy, to the energy of God - the causal law will continue to influence mankind. As long as the individual - and seen as a whole, all of mankind - does not come to his senses and turn back, this means, as long as he does not apply the given laws of God, the individual and thus, all of mankind, will continue to create further causes. All of mankind - all peoples - will have to suffer under these causes.

The two macrocosms, the computers of the purification planes and of matter, as well as the atmospheric chronicle, can hardly store any more negative energy, because the positive potential is mostly used up, that is, transformed down. Since the computers send the data to their programmers, that is, to people, faster and faster, all of mankind - every individual - experiences itself what it has sown. To experience oneself means that every individual receives back what he has input. He experiences it in and on himself, in the form of suffering, illness, infirmity, hunger or death, ruin and much more.

The causal computer cleans up. The effects break in over mankind

The image of this world today is a world which has been created by generations, made up of the reflections of countless people of varying generations, who came over and over again and helped shape the condition of the world.

In our time we are witnessing the causal computer cleaning up the earth - the causes produce the effects. Everywhere in this world we see the decline, through terror, destruction of establishments, plundering, wars, manslaughter, natural disasters, illness, hunger, pestilence and much more.

The burning oil wells in Kuwait, which triggered a natural disaster of the greatest proportions, as well as the many leaks in oil tankers whose contents have poured into the oceans, are the effects of formerly created causes. Let us also think about the polluted sewages with their many harmful substances, under which the plants and animals suffer, and about the earth's ozone layer that is becoming thinner and thinner.

Each one of us has to ask himself the question: How long can man continue to live under these escalating effects? When we unwind the entire film reel of our causes, then we can say: The conditions are intolerable; life in such density on this earth is possible only in a limited way - even though the geneticists want to interfere in the ingenious creation of God with their manipulations of genes, in order to save what can still be saved, as they believe.

Our old world that we were once so proud of is perishing. Many peoples, that is, countless generations, have shaped it and contributed to the fact that this density, this sinful world, is now dissolving. With the word "world," we do not mean the earth, but all the establishments that were created by people out of materialistic thinking and striving, out of egocentricity. And so, this world consists of the limiting "mine and me," of wanting to possess and to have, of coercion, dictatorship, power, slavery and much more.

Illnesses, too, which the physicians can no longer diagnose, are increasing in number and extent. They suddenly break in over the individual, because the capacity of the causal computer has been exceeded and the person has rejected all warnings.

A severe illness can build up over generations, when a person's soul, which keeps coming back, continues to sin there, where it had stopped as a human being in former existences. One day, it will come to the fact that the stars will, like the clouds, so to speak, rain down the causes onto the soul and onto the person who has clouded, that is, burdened, his soul. It can be that the effect of a great guilt comes to fruition only in the second, third or fourth incarnation. When this happens is determined by the circulation of the causal stream, the causal law, in which the causes of every person are stored.

The time of harvest. Without the path of recognition and clearing up of causes: Expiation

The language of the heavens is the language of pictures, in which color, form, fragrance and sound find their expression. It is similar on matter. Our world of sensations, feelings and thoughts, our words and deeds, also consist of pictures, which bear tone, color, fragrance and sound in themselves.

The spiritual life is the Being, because every spirit being lives in the Being, in the pure law, God. On the other hand, every person lives his personal being from which his individual life is formed and which is recorded as on a film reel. This film reel carries the causal pictures, which now show themselves more and more to each one who created them, because the causal computer is in the process of cleaning up. Now is the time of harvest - it is no longer the time of maturing, in which admonishments and warnings were given to all of mankind.

The divine communication, the divine language, as it were, takes place in pictures. The life of every individual person and the human language also takes place in pictures.

That which is in heaven is also on the earth - only reversed, transformed down and drawn into the world of sin. For instance, an illness consists of one or more picture complexes, of various causes that are summed up as one cause, as one picture or sequence of pictures in the causal computer. And so, an illness is our illness picture, a complex or complexes of our human aspects. An illness is bound energy.

When our causes break in over us, when we fall ill, then, this starts from the causal computer, taking place via our soul into the body. The complex or the complexes in the soul begin to vibrate due to the irradiation of the stars. And so, a wave-like movement develops. These waves - that is, vibrations - discharge in the body and cause in the cells, organs and blood circulation what we have caused, an energy blockage.

Thus, what the person has to bear is his cause that now has become active. Every person is marked solely by what he himself has previously drawn as a picture through his way of feeling, sensing, thinking, speaking and acting, through quarrel, strife, envy, animosity, through pressing desires, through passions and longings.

The soul in the earthly garment is in the school of life called earth, in order to recognize its causes and to give them up with Christ on the path of repentance, of clearing things up and making amends, and then of no longer committing the humanness that has been recognized. If we do not change our ways while in the effect, in the illness, for example, that is, if we do not walk the path of repentance and clearing up, we will create still more causes via our illness picture. Through this, we can expand our illness complex or create a new complex that is similar to our illness, for example, accidents, infirmity, hunger and the like. After a certain period of time - and this runs its course faster and faster - what we have entered into our soul and into the causal computer comes toward us again. And so, we remain in the cycle of cause and expiation.

Because the causal computer can hardly take in any more data, it is possible that the causes newly created by us come to fruition immediately, so that one illness is followed by another, or by an accident or infirmity, or the illness becomes worse and attacks more organs - depending on what we have newly created, that is, entered into the computer.

When we fall into infirmity, because more and more organs become incapable of functioning, so that the cells can hardly communicate anymore with the material cosmos, then it means that the physical body is gradually dying.

And so, because this world is heading toward the abyss, great numbers of people, animals and plants are already beginning to die on the earth. Soon whole peoples will pass away, because the causal computer is discharging. This means that also many stars will collapse when there is hardly any more communication with this planet, because the earth is ridding itself of the causes.

When stars collapse, this energy transforms into another energy, perhaps into stand-by energy, in order to be born anew - when many souls incarnate, that is, when many people are born, or when animals and plants come into being again.

The cosmic mass graves, which we have already mentioned, consist of collapsed stars which have an unimaginably great density. They are the so-called black holes. A part of this mass of highly dense material can also be transformed, that is, changed from negative into positive energy, and can thus gradually reach assimilation into the energy of God. For God, the life, is present in everything and is thus also the One who transforms the negative into the positive.

Another part consists of the so-called stand-by energy. One or several new material stars then develop out of this energy potential. New repository stars, in turn, can develop out of supernovas. But the prerequisite is that on the earth human bodies can be procreated again and that animals and plants can multiply.

According to the law of God, it is said: Save life - but do not prolong life. Because many interferences in the physical body and medicines as well have the purpose of prolonging life, we will soon find that these interferences and medicines can hardly help anymore, because the cosmic radiation is changing in a fundamental way and has a corresponding influence on people and on medicines.

The one who has become familiar with the law of sowing and reaping, that is, the law of sending and receiving, is aware that the physical body cannot become healthy solely through interferences, operations, radiations and medicines, because every illness has a spiritual, that is, a cosmic cause. For the causes that have led to the illness are stored in the soul as well as in the causal computer.

Everything that happens to a person - for instance, a blow of fate, suffering, hunger, need, illness, infirmity - enters the body by way of the causal computer and the soul. As a result of this, neither the soul nor the causal computer can be stopped by interfering in the body, nor can the body be healed with radiation and medicine. Relief can be obtained in this way, but never a healing.

Many a person has the illusion that he is not ill, but he already has his illness in himself. It is simply not yet active and thus does not show itself as an illness picture. And so, to be ill means not only to feel that one is ill, but also to already bear the inactive illness picture in oneself.

And in the long run, not even modern genetic engineering can accomplish anything; on the contrary, man will burden himself even more through gene manipulation. And so, we cannot remove our causes through operations on our body, nor by the manipulation of our genetic make-up.

A good physician can bring relief, but can never undertake a deep healing on his own. This can take place only together with the patient, who starts on the life path of self-recognition and of clearing up his recognized human aspects. And it is never the human being who heals. It is always the Inner Physician and Healer, Christ, who brings about true healing by way of the divine life forces in the person.

Strong medicines can push an illness back into the soul. But that which is pushed away is not removed. What is pushed to the side will break out again - either in the person in this earthly existence or in the soul in the spheres of purification or in future incarnations, if the soul can seek out a new body, that is, provided there is still a possibility for this soul to incarnate.

The divine heritage of a person is his spiritual body; his satanic heritage is the causes that he, himself, has created

The causal computer is fully active. Time is rushing on. The years fly by and point to the decline of the world.

Through the increased outpouring out of negative energy from the causal computer, impulses are given for great migrations of people, so that many people may meet each other in a short period of time, in order to be able to clear up with one another what binds them to each other. Many nations suffer under the severest crises, under hunger and civil war; discord and hatred work together; pestilence and illnesses of all kinds sweep the people away.

This world is still the stronghold of the demons. The earth is their headquarters, on which the victor will show Himself - when the conquered one has lost his power.

The demons haven't given up yet. They think they have to play their last trump, in order to bring God to His knees. The opponents of God have long since prepared for this over generations. It is genetic engineering.

The researchers and scientists came throughout the generations, they did their research, tested and constructed, until it now seems to be usable over a broad spectrum: the manipulation of the hereditary material of human beings, animals and plants and the transplantation of hereditary parts, that is, of gene fragments.

The opponent of God still thinks he can defeat God, the All-law. From the beginning of the Fall, he, the demon, and his accomplices reversed the gift on loan from God, a part of the divine energy, for unlawful purposes. What was white, that is, pure, was made black, that is, sinful, by the opponent.

The part of the energy of divine order on loan,
he turned into disorder;
from the divine will that makes one free,
he constructed self-will and coercion.
The divine wisdom, he turned into intellect;
the divine earnestness, he turned into frivolity;
the divine patience, into impatience;
the selfless, divine love, into self-love;
the divine mercy,
into pitilessness and mercilessness.

The impure is the causal law, into which every person entered and still enters his share, his causes, in order to receive them again.

The seven basic powers of God are the divine law that God gave to every divine being as spiritual heritage. The divine heritage, the compressed divine law, is the spiritual body of all pure beings. The reversed life forces on loan from the seven basic powers of God are the satanic, and are the heritage of every person, if he has violated these divine spiritual principles.

The satanic heritage, the causes, is reversed, condensed, divine energy, which every person has created in accordance with his violations of the law of God, and which he has stored accordingly many times. Through the radiations of what is stored, the causes in the soul become active and, starting from the soul, they also become active in the genes of the person.

Every cause is a part of the human hereditary make-up, which consists of one or more programs. Thus, it is the hereditary material of every single person. The life of the individual takes its course in accordance with the causes, the created programs, the hereditary material.

Since everyone should recognize and clear up his humanness, his sinfulness, that is, his personal genetic make-up, in order to find his way back to his origin, to his divine heritage, to the seven basic powers of God, he has to walk the path of self-recognition and of clearing up his sinfulness.

When he no longer does what he has recognized in himself - his causes - then he creates a new life program for himself, perhaps with higher ideals and values. In this way, he gradually finds his way to his divine heritage, because with the Christ Spirit he again turns his sinfulness, his satanic heritage, a part of the reversed seven basic powers of God, back into the positive, into the divine, by living more and more according to the divine laws.

The physical hereditary material became more and more burdened, because the masses of people did not and do not accomplish the principle of turning back from the satanic heritage to the divine heritage and the individual person thus continued to create more and more causes. This burdening now comes into effect.

The goal of the demons: a new material macrocosm

The causal computer is emptying. This means that more and more "black holes" will develop in the material storage system. The black holes, which can be compared to a vacuum cleaner, absorb those stars that have hardly any communication left with the earth, with people, plants, animals and stones, because their life is being taken back. Through this, many repository planets will no longer be needed.

Many people are dying because of deformed and damaged hereditary material, and many already bear the sign of death in their blood. Many species of animals and plants, too, are dying out, since they can no longer live on the polluted earth and under the ozone layer that is becoming thinner and thinner.

Because of the changing material macrocosm, the opponent of God is getting into a predicament. Just as he always seized the heavenly principles, turned them around and in their negative reversed state made use of them for himself, now he wants to seize the promise of God, too, which says: "I will create a new heaven and a new earth." Because he has succeeded in reversing the energy on loan from God until now, he thinks that he can manage to create a new heaven and a new earth, with new human beings, plants and animals.

Just as the demon has manipulated with the help of God's energy up until now, he now thinks that with gene manipulation he can establish a new kingdom on earth with human beings, animals and plants - his kingdom - and at the same time a new material macrocosm. For by creating new human beings and nature kingdoms, a new material macrocosm must also be formed, because everything is based on communication. The demon knows this, and he works with this knowledge. Nevertheless, his calculation will not work out - because God is the great One, the absolute One. He is above a limited consciousness.

The adversary of God thinks that he has to become active on earth by way of gene manipulation, in order to create new programs, so that out of the black holes, out of the stand-by energy, new stars will emerge again with the programs of those people whom he had manipulated or which a manipulated, soulless humanity sends out. The same is true for manipulated animals and plants and for new creations in the nature kingdoms through the manipulation of the genes.

Let us bring to mind all that can happen through the manipulation of the physical genetic make-up. I repeat: The demon believes that he can build up a new cosmic computer with this last gene manipulation "prelude" before the decline of this world. His plan is to emit toward the stand-by energy contained in the black holes of the material cosmos, by using gene manipulation - for every manipulation also bears the principle of sending and receiving - in order to prepare a new material macrocosm.

Hereditary information – The sending potential of the personal life of a person

The genes carry the hereditary information of the cells. They are found in the nucleus of the cell, in the chromosomes. All genes are carriers of information, of the corresponding potential of sending and receiving. This potential, this information, is programs which the person has created through his wrongdoing, through his sinful life. According to its hereditary information, the cell sends and receives and beyond it, the soul, and the causal computer, in turn, as well.

The human hereditary material can be compared to an extensive library with billions of individual letters, that is, genetic information, genetic building blocks. Every single cell, which carries the building blocks of our genetic make-up, sends and receives. And so, we can more or less imagine how many programs we, as human beings, have created for ourselves!

This chain of information has formed in the course of the development of human beings. They came into being through the first Fall-thought, through the negativities, which then became information, that is, programs, in the soul. When the human being had then become so well-structured that he was capable of procreation, a soul - for instance, a Fall-being - incarnated and radiated the information it brought with it into the developing physical body in the womb of the mother.

The same still happens today. The soul incarnates and radiates the information it brings with it, the positive and the negative, into the embryo that is gradually developing into a physical shell for the soul. What is stored in the soul becomes the genetic make-up of the small human being. The parents, too, have their share in the make-up of the cell structure and of the genetic material of the embryo.

And so, the genes bear all the information, the sending potential of the personal life, the burdens of the soul and also its light-filled aspects. All predispositions and capabilities that a person has acquired in this life or in former incarnations become his genetic make-up. The professional abilities, knowledge that has been learned and applied in artisan work, in business, science, theology, the abilities of a physician or the talents of a musician or a singer come either from the hereditary information of the person or go into the hereditary substance as hereditary information - when the person concerned has practiced accordingly.

And so, what the person has acquired in previous existences is the genetic make-up that he brings with him. What he adopts in this life or what he continues to do based on his predispositions and capabilities becomes his genetic make-up. Thus, it is programs over and over again, information, that sends and receives.

All hereditary information comes from the soul and from the person or goes into the hereditary predispositions again through the application of the hereditary impulses, becoming further programs there. The physical hereditary predispositions are stored in the particle structure of the soul and also the stars. And so, the sending potential of the individual person is widely diversified.

I repeat: What a person has thought about and carried out in the course of his earthly development and lived out with passion is, like many other things, recorded in his hereditary material. The physical genetic make-up of a person also registers his acts of violence, hatred, envy, animosity, strife and even murder or manslaughter in their eventuality. These are then registered by the soul in its particle structure and through this, they are registered by the stars.

Everything is information and everything is stored.

Impulse-givers for information: Repository stars of the material cosmos and of the purification planes

If there is genetic information, then the impulses have to come from one or more sources. An example: When we want to take a book out of the library, then we will look for the book. But first we have to know which book we want to take out of the library. In this example, are we the sole impulse giver - or where do the impulses come from that say something like: "Reach for this or that book"?

We human beings believe that we think logically all on our own. For many, this is no question, because they are of the opinion that these impulses for their thoughts come from their brain, because this is the control center of our body.

The one who has read the previous explanations conscientiously knows that the impulses do not come from the brain, but are only transferred through the brain. Many think that the brain is independent, autonomous, that it obeys only the will of the person.

But according to the principle of sending and receiving, everything consists of communication. As a result of this, there is nothing that is independent. The principle of sending and receiving is the basis of everything. Our brain consists of cells. These living building blocks contain countless data, that is, programs, that send and receive.

The whole of infinity is a living organism, which every human being, every component of man and every component of nature is a part of. The life of this huge organism comes from God, because God is life.

Nothing is capable of living on its own, because it has no independent energy. Everything is capable of living only because the energy, God, maintains the whole. God is the maintaining life energy, even in the spheres of the Fall. The maintaining life energy is also in the sending potential of every single person, in his human aspects, in his world of communication, which is stored in the causal computer.

The carrier of life and the life itself is God. The one who has no communication with God communicates solely with what he has entered into the causal computer. The one who is not aligned with God in his way of thinking and living, thus receives the impulses, "his" ideas, "his" thoughts, "his" notions, from the causal computer - but not from God.

When science now speaks of gene manipulation, we have to ask ourselves the question: Who is the impulse giver? Where do the impulses that want to change the genetic material come from?

Let's go back to the principle of sending and receiving. In every gene, that is, in every cell, there are infinitely many programs. They are the information that we have acquired in different lives on earth, for what the soul has stored and brings again into a new earthly garment is then also the genetic material of the person.

The programs in our brains cells consist of what we have learned and what we have acquired. More programs in our brain were built up by us in accordance with the radiation of our soul, that is, the impulses of our soul, because the soul sends unceasingly into and through our body. These programs are approximately the same as our genetic material. Insofar as they are active, they are our sending potential.

Consciously or unconsciously, we also take in impulses by way of the repository stars or from people or things that we perceive via our senses. When we preoccupy ourselves with this for some time, then either we activate a program that is already present in our brain and build on it, or we create new programs that also go their way via the soul into the stars. That which we don't need right away - that is, what we don't need every day - the brain puts into a deeper layer, into the subconscious. But what remains stored in the brain, in the consciousness and subconscious, also goes into the genetic material and into the soul and the repository planets. As a result of this, the impulses that become active in our brain come out of spheres or regions of the stars where our feelings, sensations, thoughts, words, deeds, our passions, longings, desires, our aptitudes, professional experiences, inventions and the like are stored.

The human being, a gigantic sending and receiving station. Gene manipulation: Outside programs cover over the physical genetic make-up and the divine heritage

The whole of infinity takes it course in rhythms, as does everything that we have entered into the planets, and thus our life as well. Through the continuous movement of the All, our inputs, that which is stored in the planets, begins to vibrate. It then also vibrates in our soul, and is transferred to our brain and from our brain to our genes. This is the information about which we often say, "What did I think just now?" or "These thoughts are ingenious." They could be building blocks for an invention or for another scientific activity.

Now we recognize the whole cycle, beginning with the first Fall-thought, wanting to be like God, all the way to the human being - from the human being into the causal computer, from the causal computer into the soul, from the soul into the brain of the person and from the brain into the genes.

This chain of countless impulses influences our hereditary material over and over again. Thus, every gene has a large sending and receiving potential, depending on what the person has sensed, felt, thought, spoken and how he has acted. From this, we can conclude that the whole person is a gigantic sending and receiving station.

Similar to a planet that orbits in the firmament, a person sends out an unimaginable number of programs. This means that the human being - who consists of countless programs, including those of his genes - absorbs radiation and information like a sophisticated radio receiver.

The spiritual law says: Everything is contained in all things. Accordingly, the processes of the nature kingdoms are programmed in the soul of the person and in the physical body. And so, certain bits of information convert into chemical programs which, in turn, cause the metabolism to take place in the body.

The human being is a nature body. He is in communication with nature. The soul is a spiritual body. It communicates with what it has stored: If something divine is active in it, then it communicates with the divine macrocosm. If it has stored something non-divine, that is, something sinful, then it is in communication with the macrocosm of the purification planes and with the material cosmos, if, through its behavior as a human being, it predetermines its reincarnation, that is, it does not strive toward the divine.

There is a natural order in the soul as well as in the body. The natural order in the physical body sees to it that the metabolism functions according to certain rules. A similar course of events takes place in the animals, plants and so forth. When this controlling cycle is disturbed, then this has unforeseeable consequences for the person and the soul, and ultimately for life on earth.

If the controlling cycle is disturbed by, for instance, the interference of man in the genes, then this has its effect on the sending and receiving station, man. The human being then automatically absorbs outside programs, for example, programs from other people or, via his food, programs from manipulated animals and plants, etc.

A gene fragment carries a certain quantity of information. This information originates from the living being or from the form of life that the gene fragment was taken from. If such a gene fragment is now implanted into a person, for instance, to heal him of cancer, then this information, these programs, do have their effect on the illness; the person's body may become healthy. But the soul keeps the programs of the illness, which is not erased in the cosmic memory system either.

These genetic outside programs that, for example, are meant to heal cancer, now form a sending and receiving potential in the person, which is not a part of the causes of the person, which is not a part of his nature. This means that such a person becomes foreign to his nature or deviant to his nature, depending on which sending potential the gene fragments carry. These programs that the person has taken in are also stored in the All and are in communication with the living being or with the life form or with parts of the life forms from which they were taken. Gene fragments are taken from plants, as well as from animals and people - it goes so far that they take genes from mummies!

In this way, man is influenced by impulses foreign to his nature. This outside control, which influences the brain of the person, creates outside programs in a person who has been manipulated. This outside radiation potential also goes into his soul and from there into the stars. Through this cycle, the manipulated person comes into contact with those forms of life or energies from which the gene fragments were taken. At the same time, these outside programs overlay the person's own causes. In time, the person also feels, thinks, speaks and acts in accordance with the gene programs that were implanted into him.

In this way, the physical hereditary material is also influenced, or it is overlaid. At the same time, the divine heritage is thus covered over. This means that the person, who is now controlled by outside programs, comes only with great difficulty to his own causes, to his own sinfulness, in order to be able to clear them up.

We have heard that the human being is in the school of life called earth in order to recognize and to clear up his human heritage, his burdening programs, thus finding his spiritual heritage again.

For example, if species of plants, of vegetables, slaughtered animals and the like are manipulated, that is, if their genes are interfered with, then these, too, become foreign to their nature. When a person consumes such products, then he also takes in components of these manipulations. In this way, he manipulates himself via food, drink and other things. This, too, has the result that only with great difficulty can he find his way to his physical heritage, to his causes, in order to clear them up, so that he may reach his divine heritage again, and thus become divine again.

The demonic plan: the controllable human being who no longer knows himself

Many scientists who occupy themselves with the genetic make-up of human beings say that it is very bad, that it must be improved.

This statement is correct. The genetic material has degenerated because many people have sinned so much that they - said with human words - are bad, and thus their genetic components, as well.

Should the scientific conception prevail in being able to change the world by improving the genetic material of man, of animals and plants with the help of gene manipulation, then this will eventually result in a completely different species of human beings, animals and plants.

The nature kingdoms, which mankind, every human body, is also a part of, have a natural order - unless this is manipulated. The one who disturbs this natural order for matter and for each individual human being interferes in the on-going event of creation, thus becoming an accomplice of the demons.

Because the demons are against the law of God, against His order, it is their desire to create disorder in the whole world and in every person. The prince of this world wants to have *his* creation. For this reason, he commissions his accomplices to "improve" the material creation which has developed according to an existing cosmic plan of order. This means it should be shaped according to his plan.

The demon does not reveal his true intentions to those who shall carry out what he has planned. Superficially, he commissions his accomplices, those servile to him, to repair what the whole of mankind, including the natural sciences, has done to nature in the course of centuries. To many, this seems well-founded and reasonable; they think it a good, commendable task - especially since the conscience of many has become dulled by the non-actualization of the divine laws and by the dominance of the intellect.

Many scientists now have the desire to carry out what people of several generations have researched and tested: gene manipulation, in order to rearrange the damaged genetic make-up of mankind and of the nature kingdoms.

Since only very few people have thought about the law of sowing and reaping, most people do not know that the time of harvest has now come for mankind. People do not know that the damaging of their own body, the damaging of the hereditary material as well as the damaging of the nature kingdoms, of the atmosphere, generally spoken, of the whole earth, is the harvest of what all of mankind has sown.

Each and every one, that is, in the final analysis, all of mankind, has to bear the harvest. No matter what comes up as inventions, no matter what the demon uses to rescue, through manipulation, what he thinks can still be rescued - mankind will be defeated by it.

Even though the decline of this world is clearly visible, the prince of this world is still blinded and thinks that through worldwide and well-directed gene manipulation he can create a new creation, his satanic creation. The one who enters this satanic cycle, by interfering in the existing laws of nature, is an accomplice of the demons.

God, the Eternal, said in the sense of the following: "I make all things new, a new heaven and a new earth." This means that God establishes His eternal order again, His eternal creation of Being. Since only very few people fulfill the laws of God, people's view of the truth is clouded. They believe that scientists could be the saviors of the earth; for the scientists make mankind believe that they can conquer illnesses through, for instance, genetic therapy and that they can create a new atmosphere, new animals and a new nature - and not lastly, a new human being, too.

But out of white will come black, because the causal computer is filled with negative energies, since the positive energy has been used up for the most part. The following is now valid for everything that lives on the earth: die - or become. The majority of mankind can no longer exist with an impaired physical hereditary material. Even through gene manipulation, mankind can no longer be maintained in the long run.

God is the energy of life. The one who has mostly used up this energy on loan from God, by misusing it, no longer has the strength to be able to live as a human being. The bodies, weakened by illness and infirmity, with their damaged hereditary material will pass away more and more.

But what the prince of this world, the demon, is still able to do is to redistribute the negative energy, this means to take it from one person or from a group of people and to give it to another person or group of people. This demonic plan that was cleverly thought out to the last detail, in order to still use the last opportunity in this world, is still possible only for a certain period of time - as long as the demon is still able to restructure the distribution of negative energy.

Not only are outside programs implanted in a person through gene manipulation, but in the course of time his level of feelings will be cut off. The result is that he can be manipulated and, at the same time, controlled.

Because it is so important, the far-reaching consequence for people is explained once more:

When a person is no longer able to reach his level of feelings, he can no longer recognize the causes he has created and therefore cannot clear them up either, in order to reach his divine heritage again. By lacking this step of purification, the soul and person cannot find their way for a long time into the consciousness of God again, from where the pure being once went forth.

The aim of manipulation is to construct a controllable human being, who no longer knows free will and therefore no longer possesses it, because he is controlled and no longer has access to his world of feelings. The energy of the day can reach a person only through his world of feelings and admonish him again and again to turn back. The impulses of God which touch the person, so that God is able to guide him, also come via the world of feelings.

When the world of feelings has been cut off, then the person can be controlled via telepathy. This control comes from the opponent of God - for he has implanted the outside programs in the human beings. He now influences these programs and thus keeps the human being as he intended, in order to create a satanic earth and a satanic heaven.

This plan of the demons can be actualized only if the demons and their accomplices influence the genetic make-up of people and use the person, so to speak, like a toy construction set, into which they put the most varied programs, programs from manipulated animals, manipulated plants and manipulated human beings.

And so, a good person can be made an evil person, a noble person can be made an ignoble one, and a normal person can be made an abnormal one who, for instance, violates, exploits and destroys the nature kingdoms, in order to create a manipulated life, and who is against all of mankind. This is then the robot which receives one impulse after another from the demon and acts accordingly.

Gene fragments – not only in the food – but also in the air and the water

In the literature on the subject, we read how cows, for example, are manipulated, so that their milk production increases greatly. There are many similar examples by which one recognizes that animals are losing their distinctive character. The same thing can happen with a person whose genetic make-up is manipulated. It depends on which genetic components, that is, information, are implanted in the person.

Many natural products are already manipulated. Gene fragments are also found in the air and in the water. If one takes in such gene fragments and if he has the same or similar programs as those that are in the gene fragments, then they can take root in his cells and send accordingly. The fact that this already happens shows that it is quite possible to very gradually reprogram human beings and eventually to form them in a way that is foreign to their nature.

Outside programs that make the person foreign to his nature are negative programs, upon which the person builds through further sins. This means that under certain circumstances a soul may have to expiate for eons, until it finds its way again to its spiritual heritage, to its true life, because the level of feelings in the person is so blocked up that the energy stream of the Spirit of God can flow into his soul and his body only in a minimal way.

The increased production of meat is also a domain of the genetic engineers. Actually the great demand for meat can be met only because more and more animals are bred artificially. Through gene manipulation or through medicines that are produced with genetic engineering, the animals reach twice their weight with a lower percentage of fat than those animals which grow naturally. The quality of the meat is also changed with special genetic components, so that people can also take in great amounts of gene fragments while eating meat.

Based on of the principle of sending and receiving, the whole of infinity consists of a mighty communication network. Many animals are unspeakably tormented through these intrusions in their life. The torments create resonances, that is, vibrations, in them, because the animals, too, have sensations. These sensations of suffering and torment go into their genes. The person consumes the meat with these genes that are programmed accordingly. When a gene fragment takes root in the cell of a person, this genetic program of the animal becomes a program of the person. This means that by absorbing the programs of these tormented animals, a person changes his nature accordingly. Later, this could result in the person resembling the animal more and more or showing the characteristics of a kind of mixture between animal and man.

A factor of the demonic "new world order": Creating soulless people by the redistribution of negative energy

Genetic engineering is practically the "crown" of the influence over the human body. One cannot place a crown on the head of one who already wears the crown of the human ego. For the result of this would be that the teeth of the crown would soon break and the entire world structure of the human ego would collapse. For mankind is endangered not only by gene manipulation, but also by the pollution of the environment and by radioactivity. All in all, one can say: The cup is full.

God, the eternal law, is communion, that is, divine communication - not division. But the adversary wants division. The eternal law says: Unite and be. The demonic principle says: Divide, bind and rule.

God is unity, and in the unity of God is community. This togetherness means: One is for the other. In the demonic terms it is: One is against the other.

When a person's level of feelings is blocked, then he no longer has access to himself, nor does he have access to his neighbor anymore. He is indifferent to his fellow men. He passes them by and they pass him by. Programmed and manipulated people no longer have feelings, neither for their neighbor nor for nature. This is just what the demon wants: Divide, bind and rule.

Through these manipulations, the person becomes an adherent and, at the same time, a soldier of the demons, who wipes out everything that is in his way.

The plan of the demons even intends to create a soulless person who is supposed to live only with negative energy, which will be taken away from one part of mankind and given to the other part - the soulless people.

If this were to happen, it would have the effect that groups of people or entire branches of the population would die out, because negative energy is taken from them that can no longer be balanced out by positive energy, because manipulated people seldom think of God.

A look into this world already shows one example of this singling out: The poor in the Third World are starving, and the rich live in excess. The whole world is to be rearranged through a so-called new world order. To the thought pattern of a new world order also belongs a nature that corresponds to gene-manipulated thinking.

Who gives people the right to play around with the hereditary material of the animals? Who gives people the right to violate and change nature? Only the one who places himself above God takes this right for himself.

The animals as well as the plant kingdoms are a part of the creation of God. They should be one with us human beings. Man is called upon not to kill. This is also valid for the animals - and for the plants, insofar as the plant world does not serve him as nourishment or for the production of goods necessary for life. People do not have the right to kill and to manipulate. The one who offends against animals and plants acts in accordance with the demonic will: Kill everything, manipulate everything, so that neither man nor animal can feel the divine. - Is this the new world order?

Adam and Eve fell from paradise, because they wanted to be greater than God Himself. And so, sooner or later, the demons and their accomplices will fall into their own gristmill, which they, themselves, have created according to the law "you will reap what you sow."

The cup is full

God cannot be defeated. Now the cup is full. It can only come to a tipping of the earth, because what has once been set in motion through the crimes of mankind cannot be stopped.

God said: "I make all things new." We can believe this. God, the eternal Creator-Spirit, very gradually takes back the life force from nature. We see and hear that every day many species of animals and groups of plants are dying and that worldwide more and more people waste away and die. Even gene manipulation cannot help.

Even though there is still a population explosion, in the long run this picture is deceptive, because it is the macrocosm of the purification planes that still leads many souls to incarnation, so that, as human beings, they can recognize and clear up or expiate some things in the brevity of their earthly existence, which would have taken eons for them as souls in the purification planes.

We human beings have created our causes and have to suffer under them. But the animals have not violated the law of God and therefore have not created any causes either. Only the brutality of the human ego intrudes into their life and through this creates new causes - burdens for the person.

When we observe the animals, we sense that many of them are in a very bad state, that their whole life is a state of suffering. Jesus of Nazareth said: "What you have done to the least of My own you have done to Me." The animals are our second neighbors. What we do to them, we do to ourselves, too. If we believe in this statement of Jesus, then we have a sense of where the souls of many people will be one day, because as the tree falls, so it lies.

This world of today with its cruelties is the last uprising of the demons. They are still striving to rule on this earth and from here to rule over the entire universe, even over God.

When we look at the history of mankind, we recognize that because of the law of God all technical and scientific accomplishments have failed and will fail, including atomic processing, gene manipulation and other fields of medicine. By the flowing out of the causes, through which all people come into their effects - and thus more and more the demons, too, because their rulership over this materialistic world is coming to an end - these scientific works could be the last Fall of the demons. This further rebellion against God through the interference in the hereditary material of human beings cannot bring dominance over God, but only the decline of this world.

An unimaginable spiritual battle between the divine and the demonic is raging on earth. Christ is already now the victor

Each of us will sooner or later have to ask himself the question: Which path do I want to walk? The path that Jesus of Nazareth showed us - or the path that is determined for us by science? Or do we want to follow the path that the politicians determine for us? Or the path of the institutions, the churches? So far, we still have the free will for a free decision - but how much longer?

Until now all the paths that man has thought up have led into a dead end - except for the path of following the Nazarene. He leads us out of the morass of this world, into freedom and into peace.

We people now come into the phase of which it is said: The living will envy the dead. Scientists think that by using genetic engineering on the genetic make-up of man a longer earthly existence is possible. This means that in order to prolong our lives through manipulation, they interfere in the deathspan that we ourselves have predetermined through the program of our life on earth. The result is that a person whose life is artificially prolonged continues to burden himself. If he wants to die, he cannot, because, via gene manipulation, science has "granted" him a long life - perhaps a life of suffering, poverty and infirmity.

What does it mean for a soul when it has to stay, for instance, in a body for 130 or 150 years and continues to sin and cannot clear up the causes? The outcome shows only burdening. For let it be said once more: Through gene manipulation, the level of feelings is mostly or completely blocked. The person is incapable of recognizing his sins. Therefore, he can no longer repent of them and clear them up. He continues to sin, because he has hardly any pangs of conscience - until maybe after 130 or 150 years the hour of his death comes when, according to the scientific point of view, according to the manipulation, he is allowed to die.

But in what condition does such a soul enter the regions of purification? It will have to experience endless suffering in the spheres of purification. It is even possible that it is damaged, which means that a part of its spiritual heritage is no longer capable of functioning fully. The result is that such a soul has to again go through the fields of evolution in the spiritual development planes in order to perfect its spiritual body.

The one who feels into the course of the Fall-event recognizes what Jesus, the Christ, has done for us human beings and above all for every soul. For the Redeemer-spark, the light that shows the way into the Father-house, remains in the soul - no matter how the person feels, thinks and acts, no matter which burdens the soul inflicts upon itself.

Because the Redeemer-spark has been given to it, the soul can only be burdened and perhaps damaged, but never destroyed. But the demons want the dissolution, the destruction, of the soul. Through the Redeemer-deed of Christ, the achievement of their goal was foiled. No matter with which methods the demon interferes into the genetic makeup of the physical body, even when he alters the structure of the genes - the soul cannot be dissolved, because of the "It is finished" of the Son of God, of Jesus of Nazareth.

And so, we see that on the earth an unimaginable spiritual battle is taking place, the battle between the divine and the demonic. It is the final battle, but the victor is Christ!

For us Christians this means that we should protect our soul, so that our body, too, is protected for the most part. The only protection of the soul is the actualization of the Ten Commandments and of the principles of the Sermon on the Mount. Through this, we follow Jesus of Nazareth, by actualizing His teachings. In this way, our soul cleanses itself and stabilizes itself in Christ. Then the light of God in the soul intensifies, which then also radiates throughout the physical body and can protect it.

Through communication with the light of the Christ of God, the many poisonous and harmful substances will be transformed in the body, too, if this is good for the soul. Especially during this time, the only protection is Christ; the actualization of His teachings, of the principles of the Sermon on the Mount and the Ten Commandments.

So that mankind will understand the divine law, the Ten Commandments and the Sermon on the Mount, in their detail and can apply them in daily life, Christ gave us the Inner Path to our divine heritage - for we shall become divine again. Jesus showed us the path into the inner freedom.

Christ shows us this path again, because He is the way, the truth and the life. He is the only protection in this world. On this Inner Path to the Kingdom of God, which is within each one of us, we learn to apply in the situations of our everyday life the Sermon on the Mount, the Ten Commandments and the Absolute Law of God which Christ has now revealed. Thus, we may cleanse our soul and through this our physical body will also be protected - as far as this can still happen in this mighty time of radical change.

The Kingdom of God emerges on a cleansed and finer earth. The new human being has a positive genetic make-up

We human beings live in a mighty turn of time. The demon rears up with might to rescue his territory, the earth. But from many divine revelations, even from the revelations of the Old Testament, we learn that the end times will bring about the emergence of a new heaven and a new earth. The old will pass away.

The one who goes through this world with open eyes and ears also knows the condition this world is in. Many peoples of this earth have experienced again and again that after a decline something new awakens. And so, we experience worldwide the decline - that is, the collapse of this world - and at the same time the setting out into a new era, into a new epoch such as there never was before. It is the era of the Christ of God, the era of the Spirit.

In the decline of the old structures, the light, the New Era, the era of Christ, can already be seen on the horizon. A new humanity emerges with a completely new life picture, with higher values and ideals. These mark the entire structure of the physical body.

The reformation from a base life to a higher life takes place successively. The new heaven and the new earth emerge by way of the stars, which cleanse and raise the earth. This means that finer material stars emerge, just as the structure of the earth and of man becomes finer.

A new human being emerges with a positive hereditary material. The radiation of people becomes finer. The person with his higher ideals and values will shape the cleansed earth accordingly. The eternal One spoke to the peoples of this earth in the following sense: At the end of the materialistic course of time, I will shorten time, because the era of the Spirit clears the way for itself.

And so, the one who wants to transform his negative potential, his sinfulness, into a lawful life energy has to hurry up, because the clock is ticking faster and faster and the human being has less and less time in this density of matter.

The steps to the transformation are true remorse, asking for forgiveness, forgiving, making amends and, above all, no longer doing what we have recognized as humanness. The one who takes this path can still master some things with Christ in the school of life called earth. On the other hand, the one who strives to increase his negative energies will be able to manage this less and less often, because he no longer has the energy on loan from God available to reverse it. He calls up only his own causes again, bringing them to flow, so that the effects reach him faster and faster.

The Kingdom of God is dawning. It is the Kingdom of the Spirit on a cleansed and finer earth; it is the kingdom with the noble and pure. It is the Kingdom of Christ, the so-called Thousand Year Kingdom of God.

After the Kingdom of Peace of Jesus Christ, the demon will be allowed to rise up once more. But his time is limited. He will not rule the entire earth again. After this last period of grace for the demons, the earth will burst apart in many places, and finer matter will also dissolve. Density will be brought into a higher vibration and refined, until it is once again of fine-material substance, in order to enter into the Kingdom of God.

With this last act of bursting apart and with the dissolution of matter, the spiritual part-planet, too, the earth's soul, will be released and return to the eternal Being, from where it was split off and was thrown into the All as a part - for the Fall-children. In this way, the Fall very gradually dissolves, starting from the earth, through the spheres of purification, right up to the gates of the eternal Being.

The souls, too, are purifying themselves. They will again become pure beings; likewise, the stars that have formed the causal computer are purifying themselves. All their energy will be transformed - the negative into positive energy. In this way, the energy on loan from God will be brought back into the eternal Being, from where it was given to the Fall-children to take with them.

We are now in this time of radical change; that is, the time of setting out. May the one who can grasp it, grasp it; may the one who wants to leave it, leave it. May the one who wants to walk this path to life, walk it. May the one who wants to walk the path into sin, walk it. God leaves every person his free will.

This book, too, was written on the basis of free will and is offered to the willing reader. Everyone can accept what is written, can believe it or reject it; he will not be influenced.

Appendix

What Is Universal Life

Universal Life can be compared with a great and mighty tree.

Its life grew out of a little seed that was planted in the soil of this world: the revelations of the Eternal, of the Christ of God, that first took place before a small circle of Christ-friends.

The seed sprouted and became a small seedling that began to show what was hidden in its core: God's light, that is, love and wisdom.

As this little seedling grew, it brought further light: the Homebringing Mission of Jesus Christ with the first instructions of the Christ of God for a divine life among men.

This work of teaching and explanation that was called into life by the Christ of God more than twenty years ago quickly grew into a strong plant, a small tree that was rooted in God's love and wisdom. All the basic wisdom of life was given to us, so that we can find the way into a God-life that brings forth its fruits.

Ever more people drank from the well of divine revelations, and the little tree became a tree of life. People gathered to fulfill the will of God. And so, from the small seed that bore the life, God, grew the great and mighty tree of life called Universal Life, meaning: living in the Spirit of God, living not only for the individual but for all who are of good will.

The root of this work of God – Christ in His divine revelations given over a period of more than 20 years – has reached millions of people, thus fulfilling what Jesus commanded of His own: to bear the gospel of love into all the world. Two thousand years ago Jesus said the following: "When the Spirit of truth comes, he will guide you into all truth." In our time of change, He has come and guides us into all truth, insofar as we can understand His words and receive them into our consciousness.

Now, the fruit of the deed is ripening on the great and mighty crown of the tree of Universal Life. It is the work of God through all those who, attracted by the great light-force of Christ, found their way to those who are building this work of life together. It is a small people, a people in Christ that is emerging for Christ, for a new world under the sign of love and wisdom and of peace, upright men and women who daily live more and more in His Spirit. It is all those who say yes at every moment to the great Spirit of unity, of peace and of love, thus making it possible for the work of the Lord to spread worldwide in few years. It is all those who feel called to put into practice God's love and wisdom in community. Daily, they are active for the higher values of life, for the Kingdom of Peace, the Kingdom of God on this earth, that was announced already by Jehovah, and for which all Christians pray in the Lord's Prayer.

The Inner Path
"Nearer, My God, to Thee"

"Follow Me" said Jesus of Nazareth. This is a clear challenge which at the same time brings up the question: How can we do this today in the 20th century? The Spirit of the Christ of God teaches the Inner Path in Universal Life, so that we can find our way to a positive, meaningful life in God. We come to know ourselves, the positive characteristics, but also the human weaknesses. We develop independence, straightforwardness and understanding for our neighbor and overcome frustrations, aggressions, fears and their causes step by step - we practically become our own psychologist.

Above all, we experience that we are never alone, but that God is near us and stands by us at all times. With Him, we are able to better master the situations of our life more and more. Through the consistent work on ourselves by mastering our faults and weaknesses with the power of the Christ of God, the Inner Path leads us into a life of love for God and neighbor, into the unity with God.

Books from the Universal Life Series

This Is My Word
A and Ω
The Gospel of Jesus
The Christ-Revelation
which the world does not know
1078 pages / Order No. S 007en

The Sermon on the Mount
Life in accordance with the law of God
(an excerpt from "This Is My Word")
117 pages / Order No. S 008en

The Inner Path Collective Volume
The Original Christian School of Life
The Inner Path to Becoming One
with the Spirit of God In Us
7 books in 1 / 1344 pages / Order No. S150en

The Great Cosmic Teachings of
JESUS of Nazareth
to His Apostles and Disciples
Who Could Understand Them.
With explanations by Gabriele
in the Great Teaching Church
of the Spirit of God – Vol. I
255 pages / Order No. S 317en

The Great Cosmic Teachings of
JESUS of Nazareth
to His Apostles and Disciples
Who Could Understand Them.
212 pages in small pocketbook format
Order No. S 136en

Reincarnation
Slipping In and Out of the Body
56 pages / Order No. S 420en

Where Did I Come From?
Where Am I Going?
75 pages / Order No. S 407en

Me, Me, Me
The Spider in the Web
The Law of Correspondence and the Law of Projection
250 pages / Order No. S 325en

Live the Moment –
and You Will See and Recognize Yourself
76 pages / Order No. S 315en

Christ Exposes: The Demons' State,
Its Accomplices and Its Victims
88 pages / Order No. S 132en

Gene Manipulation
Man without will, emotionless, controllable
120 pages / Order No. S 502en

Animal Experiments
Silent Pleas Crying Out to Heaven
48 pages / Order No. S 418en

The Dangers of Eastern Masters
48 pages / Order No. S 429en

Your Child and You
102 pages / Order No. S 110en

For a free catalog of all our books,
cassettes and videos,
please contact:

Universal Life
The Inner Religion
PO Box 3549
Woodbridge, CT 06525
U S A
Tel. 203-458-7771 • Fax 203-458-0713

Verlag DAS WORT GmbH
im Universellen Leben
Max-Braun-Strasse 2
97828 Marktheidenfeld/Altfeld
Germany
Tel. 9391-504-132 • Fax 9391-504-133

E-mail: info@universelles-leben.org
Website: http://www.universelles-leben.org